D0976293

Skillful Means

Skillful Means

Tarthang Tulku

Dharma  Publishing

NYINGMA PSYCHOLOGY SERIES

Reflections of Mind
Gesture of Balance
Openness Mind
Kum Nye Relaxation, Parts 1 and 2
Skillful Means
Hidden Mind of Freedom

ISBN: 0-913546-63-1, 0-913546-64-x (pbk.)
Library of Congress Number: 78-73688

Editing, Illustration, and Design by Dharma Publishing

Typeset in Fototronic Continental, printed, and
bound by Dharma Press, Oakland, California

9 8 7 6 5 4 3

We have a responsibility to work, to exercise our talents and abilities, to contribute our energy to life. Our nature is creative, and by expressing it, we constantly generate more enthusiasm and creativity, stimulating an ongoing process of enjoyment in the world around us. Working willingly, with our full energy and enthusiasm, is our way of contributing to life. Working in this way is working with skillful means.

*This book is dedicated
to all those who work in
the Land of Opportunity*

Contents

Contents

Preface

For many people today, work is losing its meaning. This dissatisfaction is not limited to certain professions, backgrounds, or beliefs, but subtly pervades every aspect of work. This is unfortunate, for work is a very effective means for learning how to find deep satisfaction in life. Work can be a source of growth, an opportunity to learn more about ourselves and to develop positive and healthy relationships. If we view work in this way, we find there is really no difference between devoting energy and care to our work and devoting energy to improving our awareness and appreciation of life.

However, it is not always easy to find the way to make work a path to enjoyable living. In working with my students, I have tried to give daily encouragement so that they could more readily find in themselves the means to gain satisfaction and fulfillment from their work. These have not been teachings in the traditional sense of the word, but suggestions meant to guide them in their work and self-development. This book was created from notes made during these daily discussions and is simply an expansion of many informal talks.

Skillful Means addresses typical situations that are encountered in work and in daily living, patterns of thinking and acting which often prevent us from achieving our goals and finding true meaning in life.

Changing patterns formed early in life is one of the most difficult lessons to both teach and learn. We often believe that the habits we have followed all our lives cannot be altered, and therefore we feel that we are limited in certain ways. Yet there are really no limitations to what we can accomplish, if we truly appreciate all the opportunities life provides. We can break through our self-imposed limitations, make tremendous changes, and discover new abilities we never knew we possessed. Most importantly, we can gain an awareness of our true capabilities.

Using work as a means to develop and grow has made a profound difference in the lives of my students, and in my own life as well. I have made a commitment to work, and to share what I learn with others; this is my responsibility and contribution to life. Work has richly educated me, and I am very grateful for the many opportunities I have been given to learn and to share.

Over the past twenty years, I have had an opportunity to observe working patterns and styles of living in both the East and the West. After leaving Tibet in 1959, I spent ten years teaching and working in India before coming to the United States. For the past ten years, I have worked intensively each day with Americans from

many different backgrounds and professions, in areas including business management, education, administration, counseling, construction, book production, and the graphic arts.

Though I teach, I am, at heart, a student of life and human nature. My background and training did not directly prepare me for life in Western culture, and I have been deeply interested in learning as much as possible from the practical experience of working in the West. Often, seeing a culture through foreign eyes can provide a fresh perspective on situations and attitudes that are ordinarily taken for granted. I have felt and seen the dissatisfaction many people experience in their work. Yet though my own work has not always been easy, I have found it stimulating and rewarding. My experiences have taught me the joy of working to the fullest extent, and have shown me how working in this way can be of benefit to others.

The purpose of creating *Skillful Means* is to share these experiences with you so that they may perhaps help you find greater satisfaction in work and in life. Each person is unique, and each life situation varies, so each individual may find different things of value here to provide an impetus, a way of identifying difficulties, of overcoming them, and of moving along the path to growth and satisfaction.

When we use skillful means, we directly approach our work, take immediate action to solve our problems, and uncover the strength of our natural abilities. Each of us has this potential, and if we realize it, we can then share our insights and appreciation with others. Eventually, we may be able to bring benefit and enjoyment to all of humanity, so that all will learn to lead satisfying lives.

Others may like to expand on these ideas, to make them more relevant to their individual process of work and internal growth. It makes no difference who puts these ideas forward; the important thing is the value that comes from putting the ideas into practice, in work and in the rest of life.

These are hard times in which to live, in which to try to make sense of things, and many are looking for a way to make their work and life more satisfying and significant. These are, for now, a few reflections accumulated over the past few years, and I would like to share them with you.

I want to express my deep appreciation to my students and co-workers at Dharma Publishing for their help in editing and publishing this book. Their generous contributions of time and energy have been invaluable in producing *Skillful Means*.

Tarthang Tulku
October, 1978

Introduction

Each living being in the universe expresses its true nature in the process of living. Working is the natural human response to being alive, our way of participating in the universe. Work allows us to make full use of our potential, to open to the infinite range of experience which lies within even the most mundane activity. Through work we can learn to use our energy wisely so that all of our actions are fruitful and rich.

It is our nature as human beings to be satisfied and fulfilled. Work gives us the opportunity to realize this satisfaction by developing the true qualities of our nature. Work is the skillful expression of our total being, our means to create harmony and balance within ourselves and in the world. Through work we contribute our energy to life, investing our body, our breath, and our mind in creative activity. By exercising our creativity we fulfill our natural role in life, and inspire all beings with the joy of vital participation.

Each of us has a sense of the role work plays in our lives. We know that work can draw on every part of our being, bringing our minds, our hearts, and our senses into full play. Yet it is unusual in these times to become this deeply involved in our work. In today's complex society, we have lost touch with the knowledge of how to use our abilities to lead effective and meaningful lives. In the past, education played an important role in transmitting the knowledge needed to integrate learning and experience, to manifest our inner nature in a practical way. Today, this vital knowledge is no longer passed on. Thus our general understanding of work is limited, and we seldom realize the deep satisfaction that comes from working skillfully, with our total being.

Perhaps because we do not have to exert our full effort to meet our basic needs, we rarely put our hearts and minds fully into our work; in fact, working just enough to get by has become the norm. Most people do not expect to like their work, much less to do it well, for work is commonly considered as nothing more than a means to an end. Whatever our occupation, we have come to think of work as a time-consuming part of our lives, a duty that cannot be avoided.

If there is a strong enough incentive to work hard, we may do so, but if we look carefully at our motivation, we see it is often narrow in scope, directed primarily toward gaining status, increasing personal power and private domain, protecting the interests of name and family. This kind of self-centered motivation makes it difficult to express and develop our human potential through work. Rather than grounding us in the positive qualities of our nature, the working environment fosters qualities such as competition and manipulation.

There are those who, in reaction to this situation, may choose to avoid work altogether. When we take this view, we may believe we are pursuing a higher virtue. But rather than finding a healthy alternative that can increase our enjoyment of life, we actually limit our potential even more. For living without working causes us to draw back from life itself. By denying our energy expression in work, we unknowingly cheat ourselves of the opportunity to realize our nature, and we deny others the unique contribution we could make to society.

Life exacts a price for less than full participation. We lose touch with the human values and qualities that spring naturally from a full engagement with work and life: integrity, honesty, loyalty, responsibility, and cooperation. Without the guidance these qualities give to our lives, we begin to drift, prey to an uneasy sense of dissatisfaction. Once we have lost the knowledge of how to ground ourselves in meaningful work, we do not know where to turn to find value in life.

It is important for us to see that our survival in a broad sense depends on our willingness to work with the full power of our minds and hearts, to participate fully in life. Only in this way will we realize the human values and qualities which bring balance and harmony to our lives, to our society, and to the world. We cannot continue to ignore the effects of selfish motivation, of practices such as competition and manipulation. We need a new philosophy of work based on greater human understanding, respect for ourselves and others, and an awareness of the qualities and skills which create peace in the world: communication, cooperation, responsibility.

This means being willing to face work openly, to look honestly at our strengths and weaknesses, and to make the changes that will improve our lives. If we genuinely devote our energy to improving our attitude toward work, developing what is truly valuable within us, we can make all of life a joyful experience. The skills we learn while working will set the tone for our growth and give us the means to bring satisfaction and meaning into each moment of our lives, and into the lives of others as well. Working in this way is working with skillful means.

Skillful means is a three-step process that can be applied to any situation in our lives. The first step is to become aware of the reality of our difficulties, not simply by intellectual acknowledgment, but by honest observation of ourselves. Only in this way will we find the motivation to take the second step: making a firm resolve to change. When we have clearly seen the nature of our problems and have begun to change them, we can share what we have learned with others. This sharing can be the most satisfying experience of all, for there is a deep and lasting joy in seeing others find the means to make their lives fulfilling and productive.

The chapters that follow discuss some of the obstacles to harmony and balance that occur in working situations, and some of the wholesome values we can develop to transform our difficulties into a source of growth. When we use skillful means to realize and strengthen our positive qualities at work, we tap the precious resources that lie awaiting discovery within us. Each of us has the potential to create peace and beauty in the universe. When we develop our abilities and share them with others, we can deeply appreciate their value. This deep appreciation makes life truly worth living, and brings love and joy into all of our actions and experience. By learning to use skillful means in all that we do, we can transform daily existence into a source of enjoyment and accomplishment that surpasses even our most beautiful dreams.

PART ONE

Awareness

When we are aware of the possibilities for developing inner freedom, we can begin to open to the pleasure, health, and satisfaction that are all around us. Knowing ourselves better will prompt deeper insight, more understanding, and a sense of peace. We will grow healthy in body and mind; our work, family, and relationships will become more meaningful.

Inner Freedom

When our inner nature is truly free, we find within ourselves a wealth of treasure: love, joy, and peace of mind. We can appreciate the beauty of life, taking each experience as it comes, opening our hearts to it and fully enjoying it. Realizing these qualities within ourselves is the greatest freedom that can be gained.

Yet how much of this inner freedom do we allow ourselves? How receptive are we to our deepest thoughts and feelings, to the positive nature of our inner being? Although there are times when we feel this inner richness, we often close it off, encouraging in ourselves subtle feelings of dissatisfaction. At times, we may not even let ourselves feel happy without guilt, or derive satisfaction from our accomplishments without also feeling doubt and anxiety.

These feelings turn us away from our inner resources, so that we look outside ourselves for fulfillment. Attracted to the exciting events going on around us, we grasp eagerly at them, believing they will bring us satisfaction. But by focusing our energy outside ourselves, we miss the many internal messages from our

3

senses, from our thoughts, feelings, and perceptions. Without this inner knowledge and the freedom it provides, our attitude toward our experience grows shallow, and our awareness loses depth and clarity. Even though we may be successful in the world, a separation from our real nature leaves us without a sound internal foundation on which we can base our lives. This leads to subtle feelings of insecurity, and life can begin to seem empty and meaningless.

When we are not gaining the nourishment that comes from knowing ourselves well, we frequently turn to others for gratification. But because we do not really know what is missing in our lives, we are unable to communicate our needs clearly, and so we may find ourselves experiencing disappointment and pain. The more we slip into feelings of dissatisfaction, the more frustrated and insecure we feel: relationships turn sour, and we cannot work effectively. Far from being free, we are imprisoned by our lack of awareness, drawn into seemingly endless cycles of anxiety and unhappiness. We go round and round, seeking fulfillment, but never finding it, and this searching becomes the pattern of our lives.

We live in a world that moves very fast, and that pressures us to keep up. Most of us do not want to live this way, but we have been caught up by the demands society places on our lives. On the surface we may appear to be free, but internally we suffer from the tensions imposed by this rapid pace. We move so fast that we do not have the time to appreciate ourselves; we lose touch with our positive qualities and the strength they can provide.

Our obstacles to inner freedom are usually formed during childhood. As children we know how we feel about things, and we seldom hesitate to make our feelings known. But pressure from family and friends leads us to adopt the more narrow views and patterns that conform to what people expect. When our natural ideas and feelings are discouraged, we grow out of touch with our senses, and the flow of communication between our bodies and minds is inhibited; we no longer know what we truly feel. As the patterns of suppression grow stronger and more fixed, our opportunities for self-expression diminish. We become so used to conforming, that as we grow older we let these patterns rule our lives; we become strangers to ourselves.

How can we get back in touch with ourselves? What can we do to become genuinely free? When we can begin to look clearly at our inner nature, we gain a perspective on our development that frees us to grow. This clarity is the beginning of self-knowledge, and can be developed simply by watching the activity of our minds and bodies.

You can practice this inner observation wherever you are, whatever you are doing, by being aware of each thought and the feelings that accompany it. You can be sensitive to how your actions affect your thoughts, your body, and your senses. As you do this, you reopen the channel between your body and mind, and gain a greater awareness of who you are; you become familiar with the quality of your inner being. Your body and mind begin to support one another, lending a vital quality to all of your efforts. You enter into a living, dynamic process of learning about yourself, and the self-knowledge you gain enhances all that you do.

When you observe your inner nature thoughtfully, you will see just how much you have held in, how locked up your feelings and true nature have been. You can then begin to unlock these feelings, releasing the energy they have held within you. By being calm and honest, by accepting yourself, you will grow in confidence and learn new and more positive ways of looking at yourself.

Once your inner perceptions are clearer and more flowing, concentration will help you to direct your energy where it is needed. This concentration is not a stringent discipline; it is relaxed, almost casual. Your attention is focused, not rigidly, but with a lighthearted, enjoyable quality. You can develop this concentration at work by doing one task at a time, devoting all of your attention to what you are doing, being aware of each detail involved. Maintain concentration on one task until you are finished, and then take on another task and continue the process. You will find your clarity and insight deepen and become a natural part of whatever you do.

With the greater ability to concentrate comes mindfulness, an awareness of each nuance of thought and feeling, of each action that is performed. Mindfulness is the combination of concentration, clarity, and awareness brought to bear on even the smallest details of experience. Without mindfulness, even if you are concentrated and clear, you are like a child who builds a castle in the sand without realizing that the tide will soon wash it away.

Mindfulness ensures that whatever you do will be done to the best of your ability. You can develop mindfulness by concentrating your clarity and intelligence on your work. Simply observe how you go about doing a simple task. How do you begin? How do you proceed? Do you actually understand what you want to do? Are you looking ahead to where this task will take you? Consider the effects of your actions from a broad perspective while observing every detail of what you do. Are you aware of the effects of each step you perform?

As you develop mindfulness, you become able to observe how lapses in awareness affect the rhythm and tone of your work. When you work with mindfulness, your movements are fluid and graceful, your thoughts clear and well-organized, and your efforts effective. Because you are deeply in tune with each stage of your work and the consequences of each action, you are even able to predict your results. You become aware of the motivation underlying your actions, and learn to catch any tendency to forget or make mistakes. As you grow skilled at being mindful, you can penetrate to a profound understanding of yourself and your actions.

Developing clarity, concentration, and mindfulness can educate us in a way that could never take place in a classroom, for the object of study is our inner nature. Each step of this process leads to greater self-knowledge, to a precise, observant quality that supports further self-discovery.

The strength and awareness we gain in this way give us control over the direction and purpose of our lives. All of our actions reflect a natural cheerfulness, and life and work take on a light, enjoyable quality that sustains us in everything we do. Life becomes an art, an expression of the flowing interaction of our bodies, minds, and senses with each experience in our lives. We can rely on ourselves to fulfill even our innermost needs, and thus we become genuinely free. Inner freedom allows us to use our intelligence wisely; once we learn how to use it, we can never lose the clarity and confidence it brings us.

This freedom and vitality are available to each one of us. When we are aware of the possibilities for developing inner freedom, we can begin to open to the pleasure, health, and satisfaction that are all around us. Knowing ourselves better will prompt deeper insight, more understanding, and a sense of peace. We will grow healthy in body and mind; our work, family, and relationships will become more meaningful. We will be able to achieve the goals we set ourselves with ease. When we gain inner freedom, we will discover a deep and lasting enjoyment in all that we do.

Caring about Work

Every moment in life is an opportunity for learning; every experience enriches our lives. We are the directors of a magnificent play, and it is up to us to see that every moment of our lives is enacted with the uplifting quality of true inspiration. Work, which makes up a large part of our daily experience, is an opportunity to actively develop and perfect the universal qualities in ourselves that make life rich and meaningful.

When we put all of our energy into our work, it becomes the ground from which we build our lives, the channel for putting our plans into action. Because work continually makes demands on us, it offers us a sense of accomplishment which nothing else can provide. There is great pleasure to be found in living when we care about our work, when we take on difficult but rewarding tasks and do them well.

If work does not play this healthy role in our lives, it may be that we are not devoting our full energy and awareness to it. Caring for our work means giving it the full power of our minds and hearts. By learning to care, we can transform the frustration and boredom we so often experience at work into a source of enjoyment and meaning. This caring grows to be a powerful motivating force, allowing us to approach even complex and rigorous tasks with an open mind and a willingness to do whatever is needed.

Caring about our work, liking it, even loving it, seems strange when we see work only as a way to make a living. But when we see work as the way to deepen and enrich all of our experience, each one of us can find this caring within our hearts, and awaken it in those around us, using every aspect of work to learn and grow.

You can discover for yourself the sense of accomplishment that working with care can provide. When you start work in the morning, take the time to assess your work for the day. By doing this, you can learn to direct your energy in a vital way, and develop a clear sense of direction and purpose.

As you plan your day, looking ahead to what your work will require, let your mind travel from external, irrelevant distractions to an internal, immediate concern with the work itself. Shifting from a scattered mind to a focused, careful attention will allow you to bring full concentration to each task, and to complete it before starting the next. This way of working dispels the sense that there is too much to do, and never enough time in which to do it. By planning well, and directing your energy to your work, you will accomplish far more than you expected.

You can also review your progress at the end of the day by looking at how much attention and concentration you applied to your work, and how much you accomplished. When you have worked efficiently and well, with all of your energy, your mind will feel clear and refreshed and your body vigorous. Even if you have not accomplished all of your goals, your energy will have actually increased, making it possible for you to accomplish even more in the future.

Working well is a good exercise for our bodies and minds. By developing a greater awareness of how to work with care, we continually direct our energy into productive paths, so that all our days go smoothly and well. Rather than feeling stress and fatigue at work, we are nourished by positive feelings of enjoyment. As we learn to set wise goals, and to meet them with ease, the lasting and truly satisfying pleasure we gain from working strengthens our capacity for growth in all aspects of life.

Real growth comes from integrating and applying both practical skills and positive attitudes to working and living. When we develop this integrated approach, using our working time as a training ground, our work is transformed into a dynamic learning process. As we pay more attention to how we work, internal frustrations and confusions diminish. We come to know ourselves better and are able to turn negative situations into positive opportunities for growth. We create a new world for ourselves: though the problems of daily life still come up, we see them as ways to enhance and enrich our experience.

So often when we are faced with difficult work, our minds put boundaries on what we can do, on what seems possible; anxiety and apprehension obstruct our efforts. But when we care for our work, our involvement leads to freedom from limitations. We no longer hold ourselves back; by carefully devoting ourselves to the task at hand, we transform the situation, entering a different dimension, another realm of possibility.

Just by changing our attitude—going directly into our work—we find the joy of performing our tasks with excellence, of working without internal obstructions. Even when we are tired, we find that we can open up new sources of energy. In fact, we can find renewed vitality by using our energy consistently. We all have this abundant energy; we simply need to learn to use it well.

As we meet our goals, we discover that we have more time available. We are on top of things, able to master time's flow, to direct our energy efficiently. Work actually becomes pleasant and invigorating; we begin to care more, and this care is rewarded. Caring for our work, being really involved in it, is the secret of doing things well and of deriving satisfaction from whatever we do. When we care, an attitude of relaxed alertness nurtures and supports us. Our work becomes light and enjoyable, a source of deeper knowledge and appreciation.

When we bring about positive growth and healthy changes in our work, we are far more powerful than kings; the rich variety of experience is our kingdom. Our sensitivity is like a king's army, our sharp awareness like his ministers, our love and joy like his queen. Our depth and clarity, our fair-minded approach to life, our concentration and honesty are like the king himself. Without these wholesome qualities, we would be a king in name only, ruler of an empty kingdom; with them we are unconquerable, able to accomplish goals that bring peace and beauty into the lives of all beings. Work becomes life's pleasure, inspiring and filled with energy, so precious that we are careful not to waste a single moment.

Wasting Energy

Energy is our most precious resource, for it is the means by which we transform our creative potential into meaningful action. Our bodies and minds are channels for this energy; they determine the nature of its expression. When we take full advantage of all the possibilities life has to offer, our minds, our hearts, and our energy work together harmoniously, opening us to the full richness of life, the deep enjoyment of experience.

When we are young, we have abundant energy. There is a vitality in our actions that can carry us through any task, allowing us to accomplish whatever we set out to do with ease. Yet because our energy comes so easily, we may not use it wisely. We direct it to our personal goals, and work well only at what we enjoy, holding our energy back from the more routine aspects of work and daily life.

We may think that when we avoid hard work, our lives will be more enjoyable; we want to save our time and energy for the things we prefer to do. We may not understand that success comes from effort and enthusiasm, that by avoiding work we let our energy go to waste and deprive ourselves of the possibility for growth. Life becomes like a stagnant pool instead of being a joyful ground for action.

What we waste in time and energy is gone forever. A part of our life is thrown away; we lose the vitality that comes from direct and full participation in anything we do. When we believe we have all the time in the world, we tend to move slowly, putting things off. Though we could be moving dynamically through each day, we let ourselves float, taking it easy, drifting from one thing to another. When we use our energy in this way, we seldom go deeply enough into anything to find real satisfaction; our motivation is too slack, and our attention too unfocused.

Wasting our time and energy leaves us feeling empty and unfulfilled. We look at what we have done, and see very little, for our unwillingness to embrace *all* our work prevents us from accomplishing truly meaningful goals. When old age approaches, we may find ourselves regretting our wasted years; having squandered our energy, we discover the loss too late to do anything about it. Time almost mysteriously takes our lives away, and we find that we have achieved few substantial results.

By observing our patterns at work, we can see the many ways in which we waste our energy. When we do not give our full effort to our work, we do not plan well, and we fall behind in our commitments. We grow anxious and tense, but instead of directing more energy to our work, we begin to daydream, allowing our minds to become even less focused on what we need to do. Our motivation to work is further weakened; we look for distractions, and often end up distracting those we work with. As these patterns continue, others must work harder to compensate for us, and resentment builds up and leads to conflict; thus more energy is wasted.

Once we observe these patterns, we see that the quality of the energy we put into our work determines the benefits we will gain from it. Time and energy are resources that can help us accomplish any goal we wish; if we use these resources well, we can transform our lives. Therefore it is important for us to find the most effective use of our energy, and to take full advantage of each moment of our working time.

You can begin by focusing on a simple task, becoming sensitive to how you use your energy. Honestly examine your motivation: are you working as well as you could? How are you using your energy? Are you able to concentrate clearly, or are you pulled away by distractions? When you finish what you are doing, examine the results of your work: are you satisfied with what you have accomplished? Did you complete the task quickly, or did it take longer than you had expected?

A routine task done with all of your energy will be more satisfying than a half-hearted involvement in a more demanding project. You will discover that what makes the difference in your work is the attitude with which you do it. As you become more effective in doing simple things well, you can improve your ability to plan and set wise goals, and you can carry out more complex goals with ease.

When we learn to use our energy wisely, patience and perseverance develop naturally. We persist in our efforts, not in a forced way, but with pleasure and true enjoyment. Each experience nourishes us; our awareness and clarity expand, and as our inner strength increases, we can do more than we ever thought possible. Each day becomes a stage where we act out the vital interplay of our creative energy. Our lives become fresh, new, exciting; our work inspires itself, continually revealing new possibilities. We discover the natural creativity and intelligence of our inner being, expressed in the active qualities of time, of change, of growth.

The way we work represents our consciousness—it is the way we manifest our inner being. When we work with all our energy, the vigorous exercise of our minds and our bodies gives us strength, and whatever we do increases our inner awareness. We begin to follow a healthy path, bringing vitality into all that we do. We touch levels of self-understanding which can sustain us. With our energy focused on worthwhile tasks, our lives become a time of fulfillment rather than of regret. When we really care about ourselves, and approach our work with all of our energy and resolve, whatever we do will always contain joy and meaning.

Relaxation

Throw a pebble into a moving stream, and you will see only the briefest splash. What happened when the pebble touched the water? It is almost impossible to tell. But if the water is calm and still, we can see the flowing movement of expanding ripples.

When we are relaxed, calm and open like a pool in a glade, the quality of our inner nature stands out clearly. We have a keen and direct perception of ourselves and our interaction with everything that is going on around us. Our energy is well-focused; we can think clearly, and we are able to plan and organize our thoughts effectively. We are self-assured: we know what we want to accomplish, what our obstacles are, and how to dissolve them. We work with ease, moving fluidly, in tune with our work rather than resisting its requirements, simply doing what needs to be done. Our work takes on a vital texture, alive with challenge and fulfillment, and the results of our actions reflect the relaxed quality we bring to them. We can feel and truly appreciate the pleasure available in our work, and allow the full taste of life to enrich everything we do.

The pressures and stresses of daily life, however, often make it difficult for us to sustain the relaxed, open quality that allows us to express our inner nature. When we grow nervous and tense, our perceptions become cloudy, so that we can no longer see clearly what needs to be done. We become scattered and inefficient, which in turn makes us even more tired and tense. Anxiety and tension take the place of significant action, and simply drain our energy away. We find ourselves worrying about our work rather than dealing with it directly. Our worrying takes so much of our energy that we can no longer respond openly to the demands of each new situation. Our minds constrict our bodies in patterns of physical tension which make it even more difficult to work effectively or with enjoyment. As anxiety replaces the pleasure of work, we find we have little space to find enjoyment in our lives, and little to give to others.

We can learn, however, to soothe our pressured minds and bodies, releasing the tensions that obstruct a natural flow of energy. Physical manifestations of tension are the easiest to recognize and deal with: tight facial muscles, frequent headaches, or simply being tired for no good reason. By relaxing the tensions in our bodies, we can also relieve our mental stress. This helps us to think clearly and deal with any situation effective-ly. In this way, we can learn to increase our energy and point it in constructive directions.

When you feel tense or tired at work, sit down for ten or fifteen minutes in a quiet place where you will not be disturbed, and close your eyes. Open your mouth a little, and begin to breathe very slowly and gently. Let your breathing become quiet and calm, and gently bring your attention to the sensations in your body. Do not think about your work, or the people you work with; simply relax into your body and the sensations within it. When you feel a tense place, perhaps in your forehead or the backs of your shoulders, let your quiet breathing soothe and calm it until you sense a deep, nurturing feeling of relaxation.

When you return to your work, slowly and gradually ease into it, breathing gently and keeping in touch with your sensations. Develop a quality of light concentra-tion. Merge your thoughts and sensations, so the mind and body work well together, in a balanced way. When you speak, stay in touch with the meaning and feeling of each word, and let your voice be soft and gentle. During the day, use your soft, even breathing to sustain the qualities of lightness and balance.*

*Many other simple relaxation techniques are included in *Kum Nye Relaxation, Parts 1 and 2*, Dharma Publishing: Berkeley, Cali-fornia, 1978.

We find joy in all that we do when we learn to take our work more lightly, instead of seeing it as a chore. Work is not all that serious—it is just another part of life. When we are relaxed and alert, we free our energy to work for us in creative and positive ways that benefit others as well as ourselves.

As we move through our problems without tension or anxiety, both our motivation and endurance increase, along with our ability to find a solution to any difficulty that could arise. We find that we have discovered the skillful means to accomplish whatever we set out to do. Both work and leisure activities take on a smooth, enjoyable quality. We widen the breadth of our understanding, and deepen our ability to *taste* life, to be nourished by it, to derive real satisfaction from it. Everything we do provides real sustenance, a lasting and continuous appreciation.

Relaxation brings vitality and joy to all our actions, stimulating our intelligence and energizing our whole body. Our senses become keenly aware, responding with clarity and appreciation to each sound, sight, or smell. Our movements and thoughts take on a dignity which expresses the richness of our being. As we work and live in harmony with those around us, and in harmony with the work itself, we inspire others to find the same relaxation in their lives. We gain a vision of the common goodness of all people, and our actions contribute to developing the full potential in every human being, to uplifting the health and quality of all life.

Appreciation

Appreciation springs from direct contact with experience, from a clear recognition of the beauty of life, and the true qualities of human nature. It runs far deeper than simple pleasure or gratitude, for genuine appreciation inspires our total being to respond to the fullness and meaning of life. When we truly appreciate, our hearts open to the beauty and joy of every experience.

Our minds and hearts thrive on the nourishment and satisfaction which appreciation provides. They respond with a power and clarity that lights our life with love and deep understanding. These qualities are expressed in all that we do, touching our work with excellence, our relationships with warmth and fulfillment.

All of us want the best out of life. We want to be happy and healthy, to truly enjoy and appreciate our work. Yet, though we strive for these things, we often end up dissatisfied. We may have a good home, family, friends: in short, a 'good' life. But if we do not appreciate our work, then almost half of our lives—a good portion of each waking day—is spent doing something we do not truly care about, that we would rather not be doing. We may spend so much of our lives feeling frustrated and unfulfilled that we never awaken to the real joy of living. We may begin to postpone our chances for real satisfaction to some time in the future. Perhaps when we reach our goals, or even after death, our reward will come. But death will claim us, life will end—will we have experienced more than a moment of true appreciation? Will there be a feeling of satisfied contentment for the life which has passed?

We do not have to accept the frustration and dissatisfaction we feel about our work. We can enjoy every moment of our lives, and demand that *every* experience be rich and fulfilling. When we change our attitude, and discover the beauty that lies within each experience, work becomes satisfying and meaningful; life is joyful. This is not a hypothetical possibility, but a basic part of healthy living. We can all learn to fully appreciate our experience, to accept and feel it in our bodies, our minds, our senses.

When we believe that satisfaction will come only when we reach our goal, when we fail to work each day with enthusiasm and enjoyment, we cut ourselves off from the true joy of living. We need a dynamic approach to our work, one that offers us the strength and clarity to sustain us when day-to-day difficulties arise.

Consider what happens when we think only of our goal. We may have a beautiful idea: we dream of a house in the country, and decide to build it. We begin the project filled with enthusiasm. Things go smoothly enough, and then one day a serious problem comes up. Maybe the house is costing thousands of dollars more than we had planned, or we make a serious structural error, and will have to tear down much of what we have done.

At this point we may become discouraged. The energy from fantasizing about the finished house is gone, but we keep on building, getting ever more deeply involved in the project. Yet, as more of the usual problems arise, we find our dreams fading. Building the house is frustrating: it is taking too long and it is much harder than we thought it would be. We may struggle a little further, but eventually, as obstacles continue to arise, we may decide to give up, to sell the unfinished 'dream house', and turn our attention elsewhere.

This can happen in anything we undertake when we exchange our day-to-day enjoyment of work for beautiful dreams about our goal. It is even more disheartening when we discover that our dreams about our goal are far more wonderful than the reality. For often when we reach our goal, we find it is only a glimmer, a climactic exhilaration that soon passes. Yet we are willing to trade months, or even years, of tension, unhappiness, and anxiety for these few moments of transient pleasure. We sell our life to our dreams, whether they are worth the price or not.

Sometimes, like the housebuilder, we give up when problems overwhelm us. Even if we do continue, we resign ourselves to the difficulties that seem to be a part of reaching the goal. From time to time along the way we may feel pleased with a particular accomplishment, but our pleasure usually does not last for long. Another conflict soon arises and the pattern is resumed: it seems to us that we must sacrifice personal enjoyment in order to reach a goal. Once we establish the habit of approaching projects this way, we find that even the joy of genuinely important achievements is outweighed by the difficulties we encounter along the way. The truth is that we have lost the sense of how to enjoy the time and effort spent attaining our goals.

How can we rediscover this secret of enjoying each experience, of appreciating the details of each project we undertake? This secret is within us; we can teach ourselves. We already know how to enjoy ourselves; we simply need to bring this enjoyment into everything we do.

When we are enjoying ourselves, we are productive and creative. Life is filled with potential and we can extend the excitement of our dreams to every moment. When we work in the best way we can, we come to appreciate each detail of our work as much as its completion. Why then do we choose annoyance and disappointment when we could choose to make our lives rich and flavorful with appreciation?

When we stop and look carefully at how we work and especially at how we keep ourselves from enjoying our work, we can learn to grow with each thought, every action. We can decide to change our response and look for the potential benefit in each situation. In this way we can create and strengthen a positive approach to life. Why look only to the future for happiness, sacrificing and struggling to realize far-off goals, when we can learn to deeply enjoy every moment of our lives?

We can find even more pleasure in our work than we do in leisure-time pursuits. When we approach our tasks knowing that they will give us satisfaction, we are more likely to perform them well. In this spirit of enjoyment, we naturally take the time to plan carefully, to anticipate any difficulties that could arise. We are then no longer caught off balance when problems occur; we are prepared to accept them and meet the challenge they afford.

When we use the present wisely, deriving pleasure from everything we do, we also strengthen our ability to be happy in the future. Appreciating the beauty of each moment helps us to recognize the value of all aspects of existence. This recognition adds a deeper dimension to our insights, and renders our decisions and actions as inspiring as our goals. Appreciation can be our greatest teacher, for it shows us how to make good use of our capabilities to improve the quality of life in a lasting and meaningful way.

When we learn to appreciate all that life has to offer, and we recognize the positive qualities we possess, each moment will be vital and alive. In any situation, our bodies, minds, senses, and energy will radiate enthusiasm and cheerfulness. When life is lived like this, every action is like a soothing nectar; we are alert, deeply appreciative of each interaction, of each relationship we enter into. We can accept and deal with any situation, confident in our ability and our strength. Living life in this way brings beauty and joy to every moment. No opportunity is missed for finding pleasure and fulfillment; the quality of each experience is deepened and transformed.

Concentration

Concentration is like a diamond, a brilliant focusing of our energy, intelligence, and sensitivity. When we concentrate fully, the light of our abilities shines forth in many colors, radiating through all that we do. Our energy gains a momentum and clarity that allows us to perform each task quickly and with ease, and we respond to the challenges work offers with pleasure and enthusiasm.

As we develop our ability to concentrate, we discover a vital quality which sharpens our awareness and increases our appreciation of all experience. But it is not always a simple matter to build up this concentration. The mind tends to follow its generally undirected inclinations, and we are easily lured away from the work at hand. This means that our energy becomes scattered and dispersed, instead of being well-focused on our work. We begin to welcome the many distractions that arise during the day, especially when we are doing something we dislike.

When we give in to the influences that pull our minds away from what we are doing, our lack of concentration is reflected in the quality of our results; the less focused we are, the more mistakes we make, and the longer it takes to get things done. We eventually become frustrated at our lack of accomplishment, and this frustration becomes another distraction. It becomes difficult to sustain our motivation, and we may stop trying long before we have completed our goals. As our time slips away, and our tasks remain unfinished, we find ourselves wondering why we have so little to show for our efforts.

By learning to focus our energy, we learn to concentrate. We could do this by forcing our minds to attention, but when we try to exert our will, we usually end up fighting with ourselves. The feeling that we must concentrate to do our work makes us nervous and upset; our anxiety creates confusion, and we can actually prevent ourselves from concentrating well.

Although concentration involves focusing our energy, it is far from being a narrowing of the mind; it is a means of opening to work, to experience, to life. Therefore, the process of learning to concentrate can be far more effective when we encourage rather than fight with ourselves, when we gently but firmly lead our minds into our work. Instead of looking at our work as an enemy that must be conquered, we can embrace the many challenges it affords us. When we do this, we can focus our energy in a light and pleasurable way, and it is much easier to persist in a task until we have reached our goal. When we work in this way, we learn to appreciate even work we dislike doing.

To develop this lightly focused approach to your work, start by relaxing; take things one at a time. When you begin work, first sit quietly for a few minutes, breathing slowly and gently. Be aware of your breath as it enters and leaves your body. Sink gently down into your sensations and let them expand, grounding your energy and calming your mind. You can then begin your work refreshed and alert.

Allow your thoughts to become smooth and unhurried. Take a wide view on your work, considering what your priorities are, and what you would like to accomplish during the day. Then gently bring your mind to a single task; start with something routine, and make a plan for doing it. Set yourself a definite goal, and a time in which to reach it. Then follow the task through, one step at a time, staying with it until it is completed. Ignore distractions by concentrating loosely but fully on each detail of your work. When irrelevant thoughts enter your mind, let them go.

As you work, pay attention to the quality of your energy; notice if you are absorbed in what you are doing, or if you are only partially involved, your mind straying to other things. When your mind wanders, gently bring it back to your work. When you have finished your task, check to see whether you have accomplished what you set out to do, and note the quality of concentration you applied to your work. As you work in this way, you may notice that concentration flows naturally once it begins, and even the most routine work becomes interesting and vital.

When this technique becomes familiar to you, apply it to increasingly complex activities. You will soon become more alert to the needs of your work and more aware of how to use your energy. Your thoughts will become more organized and your energy more consistent, and you will develop a logical sequence to your actions that can be followed in any task. As you master the ability to plan carefully, to persist in reaching your objectives, you will observe your ability to concentrate growing stronger. Seeing what you have accomplished will awaken your enthusiasm, and motivate you to increase your awareness and skill.

When we know how to concentrate, we are confident in our ability to accomplish any task. We accept challenges and meet any commitment with willingness. Because we no longer look for distractions or try to avoid work that needs to be done, work flows smoothly, enriched by the strength of our full attention. The purpose of what we do becomes clear. When we learn to work well, our confidence replaces confusion and anxiety, leaving our energy free to be devoted to creativity, enjoyment, and achievement. We find that no obstacles can ever prevent us from reaching our goals.

As our concentration deepens, our thoughts are more organized, our energy more consistent, and we find that increasing awareness allows us to experience more fully whatever we do. Concentration becomes a part of us, all the time and everywhere. A walk in the woods can become a truly fresh and joyful experience when we concentrate on its details—the smell of the earth, the play of sunlight on a leaf, the feeling of the breeze through our hair. All life takes on depth and clarity; we deepen the range of our experience and learn to truly appreciate every moment.

As our awareness, effectiveness, and capacity for appreciation increase, those around us also benefit. When the results of our efforts bring happiness to others, when we share the healthy changes we are making, this is the most successful goal we can achieve. As we become more confident in our ability to help others in this way, our goals can expand to include all people, and ultimately, all of life.

Time

Time can be cultivated as our friend and helper, for it is the inspiration of all that exists. Time allows things to happen; it is the flow of events, the unfolding of experience. Time gives us the precious opportunity to live, to develop and grow, to appreciate our inner nature. Although our time will eventually run out, life will end, and opportunities will be gone, still it is time that has allowed our lives to unfold.

Yet it is possible to go through our entire lives without ever understanding the true nature of time. Because we give no real thought to time's value, we toss the precious moments of our life away without a second thought. Thinking that "there is always time," we put things off to the future, or perhaps give our time to others in the form of idle conversations or useless pastimes. We would never be so casual about loaning our money, especially if we know we would never get it back. But we believe we have enough time to spare.

The habit of wasting time is passed on from parents to children, from teachers to students, from one friend to another. We are not taught to respect the real quality of time or to use it with full effectiveness. We let our time slip by; our thoughts meander and we lack a clear sense of direction or purpose. We find it is difficult to accomplish very much in this state of mind, and as a result, our personal growth is slow and erratic. If we try to recall what we have done, our memory is hazy; it seems we have done *something*, but it is difficult to pinpoint specific accomplishments. So subtle is this clouded awareness that the whole of life may pass by; the end of life draws near, our time is gone . . . and we do not know where it went.

The dim sense that time is passing us by can be very frightening. Our lives take on a rushed quality; we become ruled by time, bending to its pressure, hastening to meet its deadlines. We hurry to finish one thing, and jump into another project before the first is finished, moving so fast that there is little time for true enjoyment, for deepening our sense of value and purpose in life. Even though we may work many hours a day, when we do not work in harmony with the flow of time, we find we have done little that is truly satisfying.

When we waste our time, it is like plucking the pearls from a dazzling necklace one by one and throwing them away. But when we use time well, each minute adds another jewel to enhance the beauty of our lives. Because time is our life, it is very precious, and we need to learn to treasure it. No time can ever be duplicated;

no experience can be recreated. Each moment is unique, a gift to be cherished and used well. Life is priceless, and if we waste it by wasting our time, we lose the rare value of our opportunity.

When we come to understand that time *is* our life, we can begin to watch our use of it more closely, and learn to use it wisely. By paying careful attention to each moment, to each detail in that moment, we can learn to use these infinite moments to realize our goals, and bring a rich sense of achievement into our lives.

We find that learning to use time well requires organization; we must proceed carefully, step by step, fully using and appreciating each moment before moving on to the next. A carpenter does not build a house by slapping together walls and a roof, sticking windows in here and there. He creates a design, and proceeds carefully with each detail, building from the foundation up, nail by nail, board by board, brick by brick. Learning to make good use of time is a similar process. Each minute is an important part of the task at hand, and must be carefully considered and integrated into the overall design.

A carpenter who was careless of the details of his work, who threw away good nails, left out a brace here and there, made doors that stuck and floors that wobbled and creaked, would be called a cheat. But when we scatter our time and let it slip by, we are worse off than the carpenter. Not only does our work suffer, but we are less than we could be: we cheat ourselves. Life is too enjoyable to be wasted through this lack of care.

To begin to get an idea of how you use your time, look back carefully over the past month. Observe how much time you had to use, developing an awareness of the value of each moment. Then look at how you used each week, each day, each hour. If you cannot account for all of your time, encourage yourself to develop more awareness of where your time is going.

When you learn to measure your time carefully, time itself seems to expand. You are able to work faster, yet speed loses its rushed and frantic quality, and your pace becomes smooth and even. Work proceeds quickly because it is well organized, and each available moment is used to its maximum potential. Because you know where you are headed, you are more able to predict the outcome of your work, and you are more confident in your capacity for achievement.

If we were taught to use time well from early childhood, so much could be accomplished! Success and achievement would not seem to occur so randomly, as if they were matters of luck or good fortune, but would be within everyone's reach. When we allow the dimension of time to transform our undertakings, the possibilities for growth and rich experience are boundless. "Having a good time" is a common expression, but we often miss its true meaning: working well, growing within, finding lasting satisfaction in our lives.

As we master our use of time, we are able to enjoy our work and do it well, and we then enjoy other activities more fully. Our strengthened awareness of time sharpens an appreciation of all that goes on around us. Our energy increases and we can share this energy with others, helping them to learn and grow. We develop a sense of being of use and benefit to others which further enriches the meaning of our work and our lives. As we come to appreciate time's value, and structure our lives with clarity, we tap the deepest sources of human potential.

Working at
the Gut Level

Each of us has experienced times when we were so deeply involved in what we were doing that all that mattered was doing it. Extraneous thoughts, small distractions, and minor annoyances went unheeded. Our concern was directed solely to each step of our task, and our concentration was devoted to the process of accomplishing it. At these times, we were clear about our goals, clear about what we needed to do to reach them.

When we finish such work, our results express the clarity and depth of our involvement, and we glow with a rich sense of accomplishment which strengthens our confidence in ourselves. The satisfaction we feel stays with us, encouraging and motivating us to continue working in the same way, and supporting the development of the positive qualities that come to light in our work.

This is working at the gut level, and each of us has the ability to work in this way. We develop this quality by opening fully to whatever lies before us, accepting the demands of our work with willingness, even with pleasure. The light and buoyant quality of our energy carries us through our work with assurance, and is an inspiration to those we work with. Working in this way is deeply satisfying; what, then, prevents us from working like this all the time?

Whenever we start something new, we may find ourselves anticipating the obstacles that could arise, and the limitations we feel we must face in ourselves and others. Although we feel enthusiastic about our work, we may also be constrained by an underlying sense of fear that we might not succeed. This fear hinders the free flow of our energy, and prevents us from fully appreciating the excellence and inner value of our work.

Because we are afraid to put all of our energy into our work, we begin to undermine the force of our involvement. We may find ourselves leaving our work every few minutes to eat something, to get a tool, to have a drink of water, to remind someone of something. Though we may realize that none of these things is really necessary, we may still continue to interrupt and distract ourselves. When we fall behind in our work, we may then try to find the quickest way to complete it, giving it only enough energy to get by.

When we look for the easy way out, we often perform only the mere essentials, and put more energy into finding excuses than we put into the work itself. Because we give only partial attention to our work, we make frequent mistakes, misinterpret instructions, or fail to meet deadlines. If we sense that we are not working well, we begin to feel guilty, and this guilt shadows all that we do. If others criticize us, questioning us about our results, we may make even more excuses for our failure to work well.

When we relate to our work in this way, we pay little attention to the time and energy we spend doing it, and so we cannot appreciate the vital experience work can provide. Thus, for many of us, work becomes an unpleasant duty, frustrating and dissatisfying. Time hangs heavy, and we watch the clock, hoping that the day will slip by quickly. Our attention wanders, and work is misplaced or put off until it is forgotten.

When we do not put our energy into our work, our whole being is affected: our eyes, our voice, even the way we move can tell others that we are holding ourselves back. Our motivation wavers, and the qualities we most value in our work—our efficiency, our productivity, and our lasting enjoyment—are affected. When we fail to use our energy fully, we find it difficult to stand by our decisions, or to take responsibility for the results of our work.

We may believe that life would be more satisfying if we did not have to work so hard, or if we had more leisure time, and yet, the source of our discontent is actually a lack of involvement in work. When we do not make the effort to work at the gut level, we obstruct the energy, the interest, and the concentration that give life its vitality. We may passively allow our entire life to slip by, achieving very little, acquiring few real skills, changing jobs frequently; in short, we may drift through life without ever experiencing the deep satisfaction that comes from using all of our energy well.

Whenever you catch yourself feeling dissatisfied with your work, you can take it as a sign that you are not working at the gut level. If your work does not seem to be going well, take time to analyze the situation. Are you clear about your goals, and about what you need to do to reach them? Are you taking responsibility for what needs to be done? Are you putting work off, or finishing it as soon as you can? Are you giving in to distractions, or are you directing energy to your work? Are you aware of how you are using your time?

When you observe your typical responses in these situations, you will gain insight into your attitudes towards work. With a clear and honest view of your work and its needs, you can begin to give all your caring and energy to each task.

Being aware of our patterns of work and of relating to others, and being honest in the use of our energy, can lead us to a life full of meaning and depth. When we face our problems and shortcomings with the full force of our energy and a strong determination to work effectively, we can fully use each valuable opportunity for

42

growth. As we assert ourselves in each thing we do, learning to value our progress as much as the results we work toward, we begin to know the satisfaction that comes from working well.

Working at the gut level is working intensely, with all of our attention focused on our work, and all of our energy devoted to it. We are able to concentrate, to apply our hearts to any undertaking. Our results are satisfying when we work in this way; we look to the challenge that each task provides, and meet it openly and willingly, overcoming the self-imposed obstacles that impede our progress. There is no reason to fear failing, for when we open fully, and give willingly of our energy, we are bound to do well. Even if we do not accomplish our goals, when we are working at the gut level, we experience the satisfaction of having used our full potential and energy.

We use all of the resources available to us, both material resources, and our human resources of energy, intelligence, time, senses, and feelings. It is not just a matter of adding vigor to our actions, or greater impetus to our thoughts or problem solving. These things help any undertaking, but working at the gut level requires a total involvement of our minds, our hearts, our energy, and our awareness.

When work is done at the gut level, problems are never major obstacles. We care deeply for the work and its results, and whatever we do becomes genuinely interesting. As new possibilities open up, we find more significance in our work. We become involved in our progress and accomplishments, inspired by the challenges and demands made upon us.

Instead of avoiding our work, we naturally avoid the things that distract us from it. Anticipation and enthusiasm color each moment, suffusing our lives with lighthearted enjoyment. Everything we do reflects caring and devotion, and the results are deeply satisfying. Work is fully balanced. When we work at the gut level, we tap the true source of creativity, clarity, and meaning in life.

PART TWO

Change

When we face our problems directly and go through them, we discover new ways of being. We build our strength and our confidence to deal with future difficulties. Life becomes a meaningful challenge leading us to greater knowledge and awakening. We discover that the more we learn, the more we grow; the more challenges we meet, the more strength and awareness we gain. When we live in accord with the process of change, we do something valuable simply by living.

Change

Rivers flow, mountains erode, civilizations rise and fall. The cycles of change are endless. Geologic and evolutionary changes, the most gradual of all, have shaped the world as we know it today. Societies and cultures have appeared and vanished, each adding a new dimension to human life. In just two hundred years the United States has risen from a primitive frontier to the most technologically advanced and powerful nation on earth. World events reflect change as leaders and trends come into being—and move on to allow space for new leaders and trends. The value of money fluctuates, children are born, people die; nothing ever remains the same.

And yet, although all of us change from day to day, we seldom find it easy to change in the ways we want to or need to. Even when we are not happy, it often seems easier, even better, to hold on to what we have, to remain the same. We choose to ignore the opportunities for fulfillment and happiness that positive action can bring. We cling to the idea that we are not capable of adapting ourselves to the demands of our work and our

47

lives; or we may believe that we have changed enough. If we are criticized for leading empty lives, we may become defensive, excusing ourselves, claiming that we are what we are, that we cannot change. It is easy to spend a whole life this way, refusing to take responsibility for our personal growth.

We do not wish to make the effort to change, but fighting change takes an even greater effort. Trying to prevent change in our lives is like trying to swim against the current of a flowing river. This way of being exhausts and frustrates us until a defeated quality begins to permeate our lives. But we could choose instead to take advantage of the transitory nature of existence and learn to participate in the vital flow of life, in tune with the process of change.

Change is natural and wholesome, not something to fear and avoid. By looking carefully at the changes that have happened in our lives, we can see that the process of change is what brings all good things about. When we allow ourselves to change, life swiftly carries us past difficult times and into times of joy and vitality. Once we see how change is continually acting on and within us, we can learn to use the energy of change to direct our lives.

It is helpful in learning to appreciate and develop your ability to change to think about how you have changed over time. You are not the same person you were ten years ago. How are you different? What were you like before? Would your present self and past self be friends if they met? What would they like and dislike about each other? How did you come to be the person you are now? Your ideals, thoughts, and opinions have changed; what has replaced the old ones and why? By reviewing the changes that have occurred, you can savor the growth and progress you have made, and appreciate the benefits the process of change has brought to your life.

When you notice how much you have changed and developed even without consciously trying, you can see how much you could grow if you made a real effort to change. It may be helpful to think about your present life in relation to the future self you will become. Will your present actions improve your life, making it rich in growth and positive experience? What will you think when you look back ten years from today? How instrumental will you have been in making the changes that have taken place? By questioning your life in this way, you can gain a clearer perspective on your motivation to change and grow.

Bringing positive change into your life can be a simple matter, for it begins to happen as soon as you decide to expand your abilities. The next time you find yourself caught in a limiting pattern, let go of your fixed views and expectations, and open yourself to all that can be learned from a new way of being. Take the energy you once used to reinforce your old patterns, and use it to handle your difficulties quickly and well. When you assert yourself in this way, you will find no limit to your creative energy, to the fullness of your experience.

Calmly and steadily go through the day, quiet within yourself. When you are relaxed and peaceful within, you can recognize troublesome patterns as they arise, and allow them to teach you to change. Whenever you find yourself in a difficult situation, pause before reacting. Were your actions in any way a cause? Are you making excuses for yourself? If so, accept yourself instead . . . and at the same time, change your typical response. If you were about to respond emotionally, step back and take a quieter look at the situation. Choose a healthier response. Past habits can be changed, and positive qualities encouraged and developed. The option to change is always open, for your growth and development are a matter of choice. All you have to do is decide.

As we change our habits and patterns, we realize that problems can teach us to grow. Yet because our problems are often painful and disturbing, our natural tendency is to try to avoid them; we seek ways to get out of difficult situations, or to go around the obstacles we encounter. But our problems are like clouds: though they appear to disturb the serenity of a clear sky, they contain life-giving moisture that nourishes growth. When we face our problems directly and go through them, we discover new ways of being. We build our

strength and our confidence to deal with future difficulties. Life becomes a meaningful challenge leading us
to greater knowledge and awakening. We discover that
the more we learn, the more we grow; the more challenges we meet, the more strength and awareness we
gain. When we live in accord with the process of change,
we do something valuable simply by living.

At the times when you become deeply discouraged
and want to give up, or when you feel that it is too late in
life to start making any changes, do not stop there. By
encouraging yourself, you can support your motivation
to learn, to grow, to use your potential creatively. Instead of allowing yourself to stay fixed in old patterns,
you can challenge them and break them down. When
you do this, you will extend your abilities and increase
the richness of your experience more than you ever
imagined. Instead of cutting your ambitions short, you
can take the energy of your negative attitudes and con-
solidate it into a focused, purposeful force for change.

Once we have seen that we can choose to change, we
can look forward to the future, really *move* forward into
the future, and grow as quickly as we choose. Confident
in our ability to develop our health and strength by our
own efforts, we become an example for those around us,
encouraging them to change as well. This support, this
sharing of experience, is one of the greatest resources of
mankind.

When we are open to change, we find that our minds are a creative source of joy and happiness, and our bodies are full of energy. Together the mind and body make a good vehicle; each is a wing enabling us to fly up to meet the challenges of life. We come to appreciate how fortunate we are to be able to use our minds and bodies to deepen and enrich our work, our relationships, and our lives.

Reflect on the values which are developing: an open heart, a willingness to confront life directly, confidence in ourselves. Life can be approached as if it were just another chore, but when we decide to make use of the many opportunities to change in positive ways, we can make our lives vital and healthy. We develop a genuine appreciation for ourselves, a sense of well-being which radiates through all our actions. When we accomplish change, we can see it, and take pride in it. Seeing the change in us, others too, will be encouraged. When we support one another's growth in this way, work is smooth and our hearts are joyful.

How to Cope

Even if our lives are basically happy and successful, we may still find ourselves having to cope with many problems. They demand our attention, and prevent the natural peace of mind that makes life a pleasure. At times these problems may overwhelm us, particularly when they arise from our inability to face our faults or failures. Powerful and disturbing feelings may arise within us, so that we come to feel that we just cannot cope with what is going on.

Occasionally we may sense trouble coming, and manage to avoid the worst of it; at other times, finding ourselves suddenly in the midst of difficulties, we may struggle through as best we can, perhaps seeking assistance from friends. Or we may attempt to escape the problem altogether, trying to find a way around it, rather than through it. Those in fortunate circumstances can at times find an escape from their difficulties by "getting away from it all," but most of us do not have this alternative. And we all have problems that just cannot be avoided.

There seems to be no way to guard against having problems. But while it is true that we have little control over many things that happen in our lives, even the most difficult of situations remains a problem only as long as we allow ourselves to be carried away by our emotional reactions. Generally, our problems are the result of our inner reaction to a situation; when we do not know ourselves clearly, we are like foreigners to our senses, our thoughts, and our feelings, and it is difficult to control our reactions. Thus problems recur in our lives because we have not learned to deal with them effectively. We may turn to others to help guide us through our difficulties, but while our friends may be well-meaning, they often do not have the answers we need.

We can learn to rely on ourselves to deal with our problems by paying attention to our patterns of response, and becoming aware of the motivations that can lead us into difficulty. When we recognize the quality of our feelings and emotions, and come to see clearly the results of our actions, we discover that our very lack of awareness has contributed to our problems.

Learning to recognize the way you respond to difficulties is the first step in increasing awareness. Bring to mind two or three times when you were upset by some circumstance you could not seem to cope with. Examine each incident in turn: just how did it arise? Who else was involved? What did you do? How did you eventually work the problem out? Have the same patterns repeated themselves? These questions give you room to stand back, to gain insight into what caused the problems, and to think realistically of new alternatives to cope with similar situations. When you begin to recognize the patterns in your reactions to problems, you can start to be your own counselor, and learn to prevent other such problems from arising.

Gaining a sense of how you respond in difficult times will help you to redirect your emotional energies. When you are depressed or upset, sit back and look at the pain you are experiencing. Do not try to interpret or judge what you are feeling; just locate the feeling and observe it attentively.

Confusion, tension, and depression all contain energy that can be used *for* us as well as against us. When we can calmly face our difficulties without trying to escape, without trying to manipulate or suppress our feelings, it is possible to see something that we have never seen before. We may realize very clearly that we simply do not want this pain any longer. We can then discover in ourselves the motivation to change the habits that lead us into difficulties.

We can use the energy of our emotions to skillfully cope with our problems, to rediscover the clear interplay of mind and senses that allows our energy to flow in more positive directions. Our emotions are really only energy; they become painful when we grow attached to them, and identify them as being negative. We can transform this energy into positive feelings, for ultimately, it is we ourselves who determine these reactions. The choice is up to us: we can dwell on negative emotions, or we can take their energy and use it to encourage a healthier response to our problems.

When you encounter obstacles within yourself, or difficulties in your work or your relationships with others, take a few minutes to sit quietly. Very gently open your eyes, and try to visualize the problem, allowing yourself to feel it fully. Then gently close your eyes, and go deeply into your feelings until they dissolve, and you are refreshed and relaxed.

Then slowly open your eyes, and without looking at anything specific, visualize aspects of the problem you may have overlooked. Close your eyes once again, and become immersed in these feelings as fully as possible until they, too, dissolve, and you feel completely fresh and new.

Repeat this process a few more times, until your negative feelings completely disappear. When you finish, open your eyes slowly, and let your breathing be very soft and gentle. Allow your breath, your awareness, and the light you see around you to merge and become balanced. As this happens, you will feel a light, clear, open quality. Develop and sustain this quality by continuing to breathe softly, balancing each inhalation and exhalation. When you do this, your body comes alive, your mind becomes concentrated, and your awareness expands.

Look on the day as if it were a new life you are about to begin. Do not carry any resistance into your new life; you are beginning afresh, with no problems or obstacles in your past or future. In your new life, all experience is alive with a rich and vital quality. You are fully connected to whatever is happening in each moment, in touch with a radiant clarity, aware of everything that is going on within and around you.

The clarity we gain when we use our energy in a positive way does more than lift us above our immediate difficulties; it teaches us about ourselves, and transforms unproductive reactions into channels for coping effectively. Once we begin to understand our negative patterns, we gain more confidence in our ability to deal with our problems ourselves. When we are inwardly clear and balanced, we have the ability to use our resources to deal with whatever may arise; we no longer need others to help us.

Once we learn to cope in this way, the ability stays with us, helping us to accept and face up to whatever happens in our lives. We develop important skills: how to sense our feelings accurately, and how to deal with them promptly. There is great satisfaction in seeing the improvement this brings about in our lives, in our relationships, in our work. Our sense of self-worth gradually begins to grow, and this in itself can alleviate many of the fears and anxieties that give rise to our difficulties. Given a strong sense of being able to weather the storm, we can look beyond the moment, and gain perspective on our lives. We recognize that each day will bring a new experience. Our difficulties cease to appear so insoluble and never-ending, for we know that we can deal with whatever problems may arise, and we are stimulated to move through and beyond them capably and surely. As a wholesome, self-nourishing attitude grounds our being, we find that problems occur less frequently in our lives. Though we may still react to pressures outside us, we can control our responses and use our energy to move in healthy directions.

How abundant our potential is to live and act in positive ways! Our inner being has a power and dignity which can sustain us, lending strength to our lives, and inspiring those around us. When we reach the calm confidence that derives from our inner strength, our whole environment balances itself, becomes light, and grows enjoyable. This is what comes from learning to cope with the conflicts we all must go through. By discovering this strength in ourselves, we increase our abilities to find meaning and contentment in life.

It is really up to us. By opening to the potential our problems have for enhancing our self-understanding, we can change the quality of our lives and help to change the lives of those around us. We know that there will always be difficulties to face and problems to solve, but by taking responsibility, we learn to cope with them. By working on ourselves, by coming to know ourselves better, and then by sharing our growing strength with others, we create a base of support that helps to make our lives, and the world, a better place to be.

Escape

At the beginning of any new project, everything is fresh and exciting. So many possibilities are opening for us, our hopes run high, and our energy and enthusiasm are boundless. But as problems arise, our initial enthusiasm may begin to wear off. The future loses some of its promise, and our will and determination may falter. It can seem much easier to look for ways to avoid our work than to let ourselves become inspired by the challenges it offers.

When work makes difficult demands on us, we may choose to hold back our energy. Because we are not focusing on our work, our energy grows scattered and confused, and we begin to float through our days. We find ourselves making excuses for not working efficiently: we are not feeling well, or we need more time. As distractions arise, we respond to them readily, taking frequent breaks or going on unnecessary errands, perhaps stopping to talk with a friend on the way. At the end of the day, we have little to show for our time. If we were to confront our work directly, we might find it far less threatening than we feared. But we fail to see this when we choose to turn away.

There is a story about a rabbit and a lion. The lion claimed to be the King of the Beasts, but the rabbit had his doubts and asked why this was so. "I am the King of the Beasts," said the lion, "because I have special powers."

The rabbit thought a moment. "I have special powers too," he said. "I am small, but I have the power to penetrate anything I wish. Look at my ears, how sharp they are." And he wiggled the pointed tips of his ears.

The lion looked doubtful. "Look, I will show you," said the rabbit. Suddenly he leaped over the lion, shouting: "Too high!" The startled lion turned to see where the rabbit had gone, but before he knew what had happened, the rabbit ran back under him. "Too low!" cried the rabbit. "But I've got it this time." Slowly the rabbit turned to face the lion and wiggled the tips of his ears. "Ahhh, now I see . . ." he began, but before he could take a step, the lion ran away.

We often choose to run from a problem rather than to face it squarely. But when we make this choice, we rob ourselves of opportunities to grow and to deepen our self-knowledge. We may believe we can solve our problems by escaping them, but our problems will not go

61

away. We may try making radical changes in the way we live: moving to a new job, getting divorced, making new friends. On the surface these changes may seem to solve our problems, but sooner or later, these new lifestyles can become as great a disappointment as what we left behind.

Running away from our difficulties is a habit we learn as children. When a child encounters something he does not want, he has all kinds of maneuvers to avoid it, such as crying, hiding, or fighting. When parents shrug this behavior off as being natural and typically childlike, an attitude is encouraged that can harm us later in life. Unless we are taught to face our problems directly and work through them, the pattern of avoidance will be repeated at school, with friends and family; it can become a natural, accepted way to act.

Avoiding responsibility is a common way to escape difficult and demanding situations. We draw our energy back, doing less than we could. When problems arise, we may claim that there are too many limitations on us to function effectively, or we may blame our inefficiency on others. We may even succeed in convincing others that this is the best we can do. Because we know we are not working with our full energy, and that our results will reflect this, we employ all sorts of tricks and games to make it look like we are working as well as we could. If we do not stand behind our work and failure seems possible, we may eventually even try to convince ourselves that there is nothing we *can* do.

We may feel relieved when we manage to escape our problems, but in reality, we escape very little. Our problems will continually crop up in other forms, at work and in personal relationships. We are running on a treadmill, always passing the same scenes, never really getting anywhere. In order to break the pattern of escape, we need to carefully examine our attitudes and feelings, and take a more honest and direct approach to the way we work and deal with life.

When we take a look at our patterns of avoidance, we find that almost anything can provide us with a means to escape. At work, interruptions give us many opportunities to avoid things we would rather not do. Leisure-time activities can easily become a substitute for dealing with our problems. Talking with a friend about our difficulties may keep us from finding solutions within ourselves. As we examine our actions and habits with honesty, we may discover that even the simplest actions can be motivated by a wish to escape.

Once we understand how we try to escape from our difficulties and fears, we can resolve to change this pattern. The next time you encounter a problem and feel yourself looking for a way around it, you can make a conscious decision to redirect your energy, to go into your problem and find a solution. Although you may at first feel a resistance to doing this, the positive feelings you will gain from honestly facing work and life will strengthen your ability to meet future challenges directly, and you will increase your incentive to grow.

When we honestly evaluate our motivation, our attitudes, our strengths and weaknesses, we begin to see a deeper side to our nature from which we can draw a vital energy that lends real meaning to our lives. When we take advantage of the opportunities that work offers us to meet and overcome our difficulties, we will be able to skillfully challenge even the most overwhelming problems in a relaxed and capable way.

Our restlessness, that constant desire to escape, will subside when we see that the only effective change we can ever make occurs within ourselves. We discover that joy and satisfaction are within us, if we only take the time to look for them. When we do, we learn to overcome the tendency to escape responsibility. We replace this tendency with openness to others, with a balanced outlook on life, and a gentle but persistent ability to accomplish whatever we set out to do. This is the way to live a healthy and satisfying life, to savor the challenges that expand our potential, increasing the benefits available to us all.

Resistance
and Resentment

When we are able to look honestly at ourselves and see our strengths and weaknesses, our openness allows us to continually grow and change. We welcome the challenges of work and daily life as opportunities to understand more about ourselves and others. We face our problems as they arise, accepting them, and learning from them. Our honesty inspires others to touch the truth in themselves, to expand their abilities, and to communicate openly with one another. A positive process of awareness and growth is nourished which strengthens the bonds of caring and cooperation.

Looking honestly at ourselves is not always easy, however, for few of us want to face our shortcomings, especially when we are having problems and do not know how to solve them effectively. We unconsciously try to protect ourselves from failure by closing off our inner vision, avoiding a truthful look at ourselves. When our difficulties come to light as we work with others, we also erect subtle barriers that isolate us from the advice and criticism that could help us to grow.

When we resist the attempts to help that others offer, we fail to see that criticism can be an expression of genuine support. We close the doors to communication, and can no longer give or receive the caring that is essential to our work and our inner growth. Advice from others can provide us with a new perspective on our situation and help us to learn more about ourselves. But when we resent criticism and defend ourselves against it, our difficulties go unattended, and we pass up the chance to be supported in solving them. Because we do not face our faults, we cannot change them, and similar difficulties are sure to arise in the future. When this happens, we may no longer have the benefit of support, for our negative reactions to criticism alienate those who care for us.

Resistance and resentment take root in us when we feel we are not being treated fairly. When we are asked to do something we would rather not do, we hold our energy back from our work. Although we might open up new alternatives for ourselves if we made our objections known, we withhold our honest feelings and resign ourselves to doing what must be done. As our resistance increases, resentment arises within us and begins to shape our thoughts and attitudes.

Our resistance can be so subtle at first that we may not even be aware of it. But it can be seen in the many mistakes we make and in the way our work seems to go on endlessly, never reaching completion. Because we are unwilling to acknowledge what is happening, we find ready excuses for the way our work is proceeding. The subtle nature of our resistance makes this easy, for the problems we create can often be taken for difficulties inherent in our work. If we looked closely, however, we would see that our mistakes were a result of our resistance to thoughtful planning. We would also realize that our work was slow to be finished because our resistance prevented us from bringing our full energy to each task.

Even if our work appears to be going well, resentment slowly builds. We find it difficult even to sit down and start to work, for we lack the motivation to take our work on as a challenge. We spend much of our time feeling confused or becoming distracted, and our energy grows scattered and unfocused. We start to look for ways to avoid our work. We seek out others who have resentful feelings and reinforce our resentment by discussing our problems with them. Though we know our attitudes are not positive, we do not confront our resentment directly.

As our resentment increases, we find that anything makes us angry. Minor annoyances can enrage us; people who question our views antagonize us. It seems as if each moment of life has been designed to obstruct us. It is easy to be carried away by an angry temper or a sullen mood, but if we take a second look, we will see that we have created this hostile world ourselves, and resentment and resistance lie at its heart.

When we are resentful, it is easy to lose sight of even our most cherished personal ambitions. This is why we say cruel things to those we love when we are angry, and why we risk undermining even our most valued goals with badly-timed emotional outbursts. Resentment, more than any other quality, can cut us off from our true feelings and prevent us from further growth.

How can we skillfully deal with resistance and resentment in ourselves? We can learn to honestly confront our difficulties, however painful they may be. When we feel ourselves resisting our work, we can learn to stop and face the situation. Watching ourselves as we go through resentment and resistance can teach us a great deal about how we perpetuate and even provoke our own difficulties, and this insight can provide us with the impetus to change.

Resentful feelings are a sign that we do not want to face ourselves and our difficulties. We can change this pattern by looking for the truth in the advice we are offered and allowing ourselves to acknowledge it. Instead of turning away from our work, we can choose to look for the creative possibilities in it. We can find an aspect of our work that interests us and direct our energy there, until the positive feelings this work gives us have replaced our resentment and resistance. Once we contact these positive feelings, we can strengthen and sustain them. Thus we transform a negative situation into a positive source of insight and clarity.

We can also learn to respond openly to resistance in others. We find that when we resist and fight others' resistance, we encourage this negative energy to build up and block the possibility of working well together. Instead of fighting when such situations occur, we can look to the positive side of the person who is resisting. We can allow ourselves to feel compassion for him by remembering the times when we provoked similar arguments and how we felt at the time.

Everyone has an avenue by which he can be approached, something he likes and cares for. If we can find this avenue, we can begin to communicate. Finding out what pleases someone and sharing with them can establish an open and positive atmosphere that will lead to mutual trust and respect. Once we have formed a firm base of good communication, we can encourage others to express themselves more honestly, and to apply more willingness to their work and their relationships.

How much more satisfying it is to learn from each other, to develop strength, to support the growth of positive qualities such as dedication, enthusiasm, and loyalty. When we develop these qualities and encourage their development in others, we have far more energy to deal with problems in our work; when we are able to let go of our resistance, concern and motivation increase for everyone. We begin to view our work as a way to grow and develop, and with this attitude, it is even easier for us to deal openly with one another. We thus create a positive cycle. The working atmosphere becomes both lighter and more satisfying. When difficulties arise, we no longer look for excuses or try to blame others; we take responsibility for the situation and act to resolve it. As we become willing to help each other through difficulties, cooperation develops naturally, and work proceeds smoothly.

A simple exercise you can practice every morning before starting work will help you to approach whatever you do with an open willingness. Sit comfortably with your back straight, and take about fifteen minutes to relax as fully as you can. Let every part of your body become relaxed, until you feel a sense of completely open space. In this open space, create your priorities for the day. Take a totally positive attitude toward yourself and what you have to do. During the day, be open to whatever may arise and sustain the relaxed, expansive quality you have developed in everything you do.

When we have the courage to let go of resentment and resistance, and make real efforts to develop an open attitude, we will grow, and so will our friends and those we work with. When we are open and clearsighted, willing to appraise our behavior honestly, our work and our life are both flowing and joyful.

70

Letting Go

We have all had the experience of trying to remember a name or the answer to a question. Though we knew the answer, no matter how hard we tried to focus our mind on finding it, it would not come. Finally, when we dropped it and went on to something else, it came to us spontaneously. By trying too hard, we actually prevented ourselves from finding the answer; but by letting go of the problem, by relaxing and allowing our energy to flow once again, we allowed the answer to come to us.

This quality of letting go can teach us to live and work with a fluid ease, a smooth approach to even the most complex situations. When we let go of problems that constrict our minds and bodies, we release energy which can move in new and positive directions. Letting go is liberating; it brings the play of creative energy into all of our actions, opening us to new possibilities of thinking and acting, new ways of being.

Because it is a common tendency in our culture to hold on to things, letting go may at first appear to be an ineffective response to a problem. The phrase "to the bitter end" expresses the value we place on holding on to our ideas and emotions. We may try to exert control over our experience by maintaining a consistent point of view. From childhood we are taught this type of control, and by exercising it, we actually learn to suppress or hold back both our ideas and our feelings. We come to think of 'letting go' as giving in, or somehow losing control.

At times, in order to maintain control and to protect our self-image, or to convince others that we are right, we may choose to hold on to our views even when we know we are wrong. It may seem that holding on to a position indicates perseverance and strength, but this actually reinforces a rigidity which narrows our perspective and prevents us from seeing the reality of a situation.

What is behind this rigidity, this need for control? When we react to difficulties in a tense and inflexible way, though we may not realize it, we are actually holding on to fear. We hold feelings in check because we fear exposing ourselves and our beliefs to the reactions of others. An underlying lack of self-confidence causes us to lock many of our feelings and true beliefs inside.

When we let go of our fears, and the emotions and fixed views that stem from fear, we actually begin to gain control over our lives. It becomes easier to solve our problems; our work becomes lighter and more enjoyable, and our relationships more satisfying. As our inner tensions diminish, we are more able to experience our feelings with clarity. Our emotions lose their control over us, for they can survive only when we give them energy. We gain a clear knowledge of each situation, which gives us real strength and confidence. As our feelings and perceptions flow more naturally, we can respond flexibly, and with an open heart, to the needs of each new situation. When we learn to let go, we allow the shape of our being to change.

When we truly let go, we release our natural creative energy to flow through every experience. We can take the energy we normally give to our emotions and fixed views, and use it to find more healthy and productive solutions to our problems. As we learn to adapt readily to the demands of each situation, and to the needs of those around us, every experience becomes an opportunity to deepen our appreciation of ourselves and others.

When we realize the value of letting go, we can begin to develop this quality in our daily lives. Whenever you find yourself holding on to a position or an emotion, unable to let go, take a few minutes to relax and let your breathing become soft and even. Then choose some task and ease into it, forgetting everything else. Develop a quality of concentration that is not forceful, but very light and gentle. By concentrating in this way for a period of time, you can begin to lighten your mental patterns and disperse the energies that are blocking your well-being. Try not to think about the problems you are having, but simply invest all of your energy in the task you have chosen, and stay with it until it is done.

Whenever you feel a twinge of guilt or worry luring you back into an unhealthy state of mind, gently bring your attention back to what you are doing, making an effort to balance these emotions with positive feelings. Simply allow your mind to contact the positive energy you are putting into your work, and let go of any negative tendencies that should arise. You will find that new energy becomes available to help you work in a clear and unobstructed way.

Every moment provides fresh opportunities to learn and grow; we do not need to allow our habitual emotional and mental reactions to restrict and limit us. We can use them like spices, to make our lives flavorful and rich. Each troublesome situation is an opportunity to practice letting go of our hold on negativity. Each time we let go and allow ourselves to change, we can take advantage of the abundant energy within us, and open ourselves up to further growth. Letting go in this way creates a vast potential for healthful living, for the means we develop to deal with difficulties are simultaneously the means by which we savor life and become exhilarated by it.

When we are flexible, able to adapt to the demands of even difficult situations, we become effective in whatever we do. We constantly learn and change.

Rather than forcefully pursuing our goals, we bring a light, fluid quality to each action that allows us to achieve our aims with ease and enjoyment. As we discover that we have the ability to accomplish whatever we set out to do, we begin to wake up, to see more of the possibilities in life. We become our own teacher, guiding ourselves into a flowing interaction with our environment and with the world. As we continue to open to the nature of existence, we are able to share with others, and to participate in actions which bring benefit to all.

Superficiality

From early childhood we are taught to speak and act in ways that are approved by others. When we are children we are naturally open, but we are also dependent, and learn by following the example set for us by parents, friends, and peers. Following their lead provides us with some measure of security; our lives seem to go more smoothly when we go along with everyone else. Most of us soon learn to base our perceptions and actions on what is expected of us rather than on what is meaningful to us, and we may become so dependent on others' standards that we no longer know what we truly feel.

When we rely on superficial judgments and perceptions, it is difficult to see beneath appealing mannerisms to the truth of underlying feelings. We may consider anyone who speaks sweetly and appears to agree with our views to be loving and warm—until they turn away from us in difficult times, leaving us unsupported and confused. When we let such actions go by without honestly confronting them, we reinforce a habit of superficiality in ourselves and others. Because many of those around us behave in the same way, the patterns of superficiality are seldom challenged.

The habit of superficiality is comforting, even reassuring, for it means that we seldom have to look at our own shortcomings. But by cultivating the smooth mannerisms, the white lies, and the many games of superficiality, we limit our potential to develop the qualities of honest behavior. Our lives lack depth, for we have cut ourselves off from the truth of our inner being.

It has been said that the average person lies over two hundred times a day. Telling white lies to save face or spare others' feelings is encouraged at school, at home, and at work. Most of these lies are the superficial responses that others expect to hear; when we are asked "how are you?" we say we feel fine, when in truth we do not. Yet adults, by their example, teach children that even 'not-so-white' lies are acceptable. One lie leads to another, and even when an honest response is called for, we may avoid making it; though many feelings may be arising within us, we hide them.

We are friendly and cooperative as long as our dealings with others remain on a superficial level; if few demands are placed upon us, we are comfortable. But when we are pushed a little past our ordinary limits, our friendly attitude soon disappears. Even then, we manage to maintain a smooth manner, hiding any resentment we may feel. But though we act as if everything were fine, aggravation and dissatisfaction are gradually building up within us.

What value is there in living like this? When we live superficially, our abilities and our feelings stay buried beneath these subtle games and manipulations, beneath the weight of discontent that becomes a part of our lives. We are unable to experience pleasure or joy very deeply; often our most satisfying feelings are tinged with guilt or anxiety. The more we suppress our inner nature, the more pressure builds up within us, blocking the flow of our actions and relationships with others. This suppression can even lead us to extreme behavior which is an outlet for the energies locked so tightly inside.

When we carry our superficial values into our work, we may become skilled at creating the impression that things are going well. When we have failed to meet a deadline on a project, we can come up with a hundred reasons: materials were not delivered on time, information was not available, someone was sick for several days. Our arguments may be conveniently airtight. At these times, even the thought of being honest seems threatening, for an honest response would expose our indifference or lack of willingness to do what is required in the work.

We may keep up an appearance of being busy, but actually we may be putting as little concentration and energy into our work as we can. Because we act and work at a superficial level, we often do not remember the simplest details about what we did a week ago, or even yesterday. We find it difficult to remember what we have accomplished, or to pinpoint in exactly what direction we are headed.

Superficiality by its very nature clouds our perceptions of reality, and traps us in a way of living that makes even our leisure activities hollow and disappointing. Because we find so little fulfillment within ourselves, we may look for happiness and satisfaction in material goods and social success. These things could enrich our experience, but because we are unable to truly appreciate them, we cannot really learn to value them.

If someone points out the superficiality of our lives, we may deny it; we may not even see it. Even if inside we agree, we may not know how to honestly respond. We seem unwilling to take a closer look at reality, and may even be suspicious of those who make an effort to live with honesty and integrity. Instead of encouraging honesty, we may reject this quality in others. Thus, those who are attempting to lead honest lives must carry an additional burden which makes it hard for them to grow or even survive.

But truth is worth the effort. Honesty is like gold; its value is priceless. When we are honest with ourselves and others, the light of truth brings a clarity to all of our perceptions and actions. As we open our senses to the true quality of life, we can develop our inner nature, and our self-knowledge leads to a new and open perspective. Even in difficult circumstances, we remain content and steady.

We lead superficial lives only because we choose to ignore the messages from our hearts and minds. We can just as easily choose to listen the next time our hearts tell us that we have lied to our friend, or the next time we feel guilty for making excuses. There is no secret to discovering the true quality of our inner nature, for our minds and senses are eager to tell us all about ourselves. All we need to do is listen.

We can challenge the superficial quality that we bring to our work and our other activities by simply developing our awareness. When we come to see work as a source of growth and creativity, we find a flowing energy that carries us through to any goal we choose. Freed from the guilt and anxiety that are always present when we fail to accomplish our goals, we touch a source of energy and motivation greater than we thought possible. Life becomes rich and vital.

By using skillful means to enrich our lives and bring our creative potential into everything we do, we can penetrate to the heart of our true nature. We then gain an understanding of the basic purpose of life, and appreciate the joy of making good use of our precious time and energy.

Manipulation

Throughout history we have sought the means to live in harmony with one another. We have developed ideal standards of behavior which urge us to cherish qualities such as love and honesty, selflessness, and compassion for others. When we are concerned for the welfare of all people, we naturally develop these qualities in ourselves, for they contribute to balance and harmony in the world. But when our motivation is self-centered, we may find ourselves thinking and acting in ways that are subtly destructive to both ourselves and others.

In Tibet, there is a saying: "The artist's brush can draw any kind of picture." Just as the artist can use the brush in any way he desires, without reference to rules or guidelines, so we can use our acts, feelings, or beliefs to gain any purpose, without regard for the truth or reality of the situation. When we set aside a respect for human nature in favor of achieving a self-centered goal, and become willing to manipulate others for our own purposes, we choose to contribute to a pattern that can weaken and supplant our most vital traditions and values.

Manipulation has a subtle, pervasive quality; as we practice it individually, it can quietly overtake our whole society. We can see it at every level of life, from the child who plays one parent against the other, to governments that move nations and people like players on a chessboard to increase their own power and wealth. The problem has amazing complexity, for it is the creation of millions of individuals, each choosing to use manipulation in small ways, to reach their own ends. Whether we manipulate others, or allow ourselves to be manipulated, each of us contributes to the slow undermining of the quality and value of life.

As we learn to equate manipulation with success, positive qualities such as honesty begin to appear naive. Gradually we relinquish the values of truth and integrity, and the entire quality of life begins to decline. Our lives may appear to be functioning smoothly; our work may be well-planned and coordinated, and we may be making efficient progress. But underneath the surface there is a slippery, almost furtive quality, born out of the knowledge that human values are being denied.

Manipulation plays on our weaknesses, touching our deepest fears and our strongest wishes, drawing its strength from our selfish desires. Others convince us that we have 'needs' that are crucial to our well-being or happiness, and we become eager to acquire certain products or follow certain beliefs. Though we feel we are treating ourselves well, we are actually selling ourselves to the influence of others.

By invoking authority in the name of an ideal, those who are skilled at manipulation may stir up strong emotions, leading us into actions which do not serve our best interests. In such situations, if we were to stop and take a closer look, we might find that we do not agree at all with what is happening. But it is not easy to admit to ourselves that we are so easily influenced, especially if we have been led to believe that we are following a goal which is worth attaining. We do not want to admit that we are being manipulated, because we often enjoy what we are maneuvered into doing, and may feel ourselves fortunate to be involved in work we believe is valuable. We lose sight of reality and surrender the responsibility to think clearly for ourselves; for when we allow others to manipulate and control us, we allow them to think for us as well.

Even if we recognize we are being manipulated, it is far easier to remain comfortable and secure than to confront the situation honestly. We cling to our security, avoiding conflicts and risks, and before we know it, we are caught by our fears and desires.

We find it easy to manipulate situations ourselves. We may seek out those who are less aggressive than we are and control and manipulate them, making use of their passivity to get our way. We may put on an appearance of helplessness to manipulate others into performing tasks we do not wish to do. At times we are pleasant to others only to get what we want from them, or we use our charm to win others to our view.

Manipulation is much like telling lies: once we begin, we fall into patterns of deception that are nearly impossible to escape. Manipulation is a two-edged sword, for we cannot manipulate others without compromising our own beliefs and feelings. Exposed to our own and others' dishonesty, our nature gradually becomes covered over by layers of deceit. Our energy cannot flow freely, and our perceptions remain narrow and restricted. By attempting to control the outcome of events in our lives, we establish certain limitations for our own behavior, as well as that of others. We find we must guard against being honest, for revealing our innermost feelings would expose our self-centered motivation. We calculate our interactions with others, maintaining artificial relationships designed to protect our self-image.

We may not even notice that by doing this we are narrowing channels of communication, and inhibiting personal freedom. On the surface, we may appear self-confident, but at heart there is confusion, in both our thoughts and our actions. For by encouraging artificial

responses in our relationships, we have lost touch with our most precious possession, our open and responsive human nature.

When we are tempted to try to manipulate a situation, it is especially important to remember that manipulation will not give us true control. Many who rely on these techniques believe that they are themselves free from any consequences. But it is not the nature of manipulation to be one-sided. Because the purpose of manipulation does not include the welfare of all people, we cannot control its eventual effects. If we have deceived others in order to gain a selfish end, we may one day find ourselves deceived in turn. Ultimately, instead of directing the outcome, each of us becomes the victim of our dishonest motives, subject to the hurt and disappointment we have inflicted on others.

Even with an awareness of the far-reaching effects of manipulation, it is difficult to face the truth of the situation, particularly if manipulation forms a strong basis for our daily habits. We therefore need to look carefully and intelligently at the way we work, the way we think, and the way we work with others. Though we may now be honest to a certain extent, when we look more deeply, we will see that there are many levels of honesty, and at each point there is a corresponding level of subtle manipulation. When we look clearly at ourselves, we can penetrate to the truth and become aware of the quality of our motivation.

Although it does not seem realistic to confront manipulation at the community or global level, we can change individually. When we stand behind our perceptions, voicing our concerns and feelings honestly, we stimulate progress and growth in all aspects of our lives. As we continue to increase our ability to be honest, our healthy patterns may also influence others to be more honest in their own lives.

Being honest can lead to clear thinking, to strength of conviction, and to an accurate view of reality. When we are honest, we are free to express ourselves naturally, to respond appropriately to the needs of a situation. But it is not easy to learn this honesty, for it may often lead to confrontation, criticism, and resentment.

When we look closely at our motivation, we see that often we try to manipulate others in order to avoid a negative response. For example, when we scold a child who is doing something dangerous, or when we point out someone's mistakes, we are considered harsh and unkind, and others may resent us, no matter how carefully we couch our words. So we often choose a 'kinder' way to deal with such situations. We bribe the child with candy to be good, or we ignore our friend's mistakes in order to preserve good feelings in the friendship. In order to maintain easy-going relationships, we quietly go along with even those things we know to be wrong.

Being honest at the times we usually resort to manipulation is not easy. We may even wonder if being honest is the intelligent thing to do, since revealing our true perceptions exposes us to the rejection of others, and may even make our work more difficult. Truth has an open, bright, naked quality which we are unaccustomed to confronting directly, and which can be unsettling both to ourselves and to those around us. But although we may find ourselves stripped of some of our working tools if we give up manipulation, we will soon find much more effective tools: honesty, clear communication, confidence in our abilities, and strength in our beliefs and convictions.

When you next begin to interact with someone at work, observe the nature of your motives; look to see if you are manipulating the situation. As you speak, notice your thoughts, gestures, and words. If you are not certain whether you are being manipulative or not, ask for feedback. Even if you do not like what you hear, listen carefully, without defending yourself. As you continue to observe your interactions with others, and develop honesty and caring in your communication, you will develop a clarity and a discriminating awareness about your own motives and those of others that will bring stability and strength to your life.

When we are honest, open-minded, and in touch with our feelings, we gain a clearer understanding of ourselves and what is going on in the world and in our lives. This understanding enhances the integrity of our lives and allows us to express ourselves freely. We find ourselves in control of situations, not as a result of maneuvering, but as a natural consequence of our honest and responsible actions.

By taking responsibility for our honesty, we also extend to others the space and the opportunity to be honest themselves, and this healthy attitude begins to spread in the same way that the patterns of manipulation have spread. When we bring into our lives the qualities that deepen our insight, we begin to see them reflected in co-workers, in our family, even in our community. Our immediate goal is to better our own experience, but as we truly develop honesty and caring, we benefit others as well. Our mood grows lighter; our tolerance for the views of others increases; we radiate a healthy energy that causes those around us to feel relaxed and comfortable. In this way, positive attitudes move in ever-widening circles, lifting up the quality of life wherever they are felt.

Competition

Competition is found in almost every aspect of life. It is the foundation of most of our sports and games, and it plays a large role in business and our personal lives as well. We are continually concerned with who is the fastest, the smartest, the richest, the best. Among scholars, philosophers, and religious leaders, there is constant striving to be more correct, more original, more devout than anyone else. Even lovers work to outdo each other in their amorous skills.

When we compete without thinking to 'win', valuing everyone's efforts equally, competition can be a very positive motivating force. It can teach us to appreciate our abilities more deeply, and it can lead to an appreciation and a greater respect for the capabilities of others as well. Unfortunately, because competition is the road to success and power in business, politics, and education, even in social interactions, it is usually used to gain selfish aims. Instead of competing *with* others, we compete *against* them. When competition becomes combat, it loses its power to inspire, and becomes instead a form of pressure which creates disharmony in our minds and senses, upsetting the natural balance of our lives.

As we compete with one another to succeed, we widen the distance between ourselves and others. We become so intent on our quest for achievement that it becomes easy to ignore the feelings and hopes of those around us. We become willing to manipulate others to prove we are better than they are, and soon the aspirations and efforts of even our friends are undermined. The enmity and suspicion that result from competing in this way can create barriers between ourselves and others that are beyond our ability to overcome.

The urge to win causes us to focus on the negative rather than the positive qualities of those around us so that we will appear more successful; we learn to point out the failings of others to make ourselves look superior. But what is the cost of this pattern? Do we benefit in the long run from treating others like this? Are we really better than they are, or are we standing on false ground? Though we may laugh at others, if we faced ourselves honestly, what would we have to laugh at?

When we lose touch with human values, we are cut off from the satisfying feelings that come from sharing. Caught up in the fascination and excitement aroused by winning, we begin to depend on the thrill of the moment to fulfill us, sometimes even risking our lives in dangerous actions to achieve these moments.

As our desire to win becomes stronger, competition becomes an end in itself, and takes the place of meaningful action. We seek more specialized areas of endeavor where we will be sure to win, thus creating grounds for even narrower rivalries. We lose the opportunity to share with others, and we lose interest in things outside our sphere. The energy that we could be using to develop a healthy attitude in our work is directed instead into petty jealousies, and we become increasingly alienated from openness and cooperation, from the real sources of human satisfaction. As long as we are caught in the pattern of competition, neither our work nor our relationships can be truly satisfying.

Competition can become so ingrained in our attitude that we believe it to be a natural human quality; but actually we learn it at home, in school, at our work. We teach it to our children, pushing them to compete because we want them to be more successful than we have been. This pressure to succeed, however, often only teaches our children to fear failure, a fear which gradually undermines their self-confidence and actually prevents them from succeeding. Perhaps we urge our children to compete because we believe it will stimulate their motivation. But motivation that emphasizes success alone cannot encourage the well-integrated development of all their abilities.

In order to succeed, we focus only on certain of our talents, and thus limit our wider potential. As long as we meet with success, everything is fine; but if we fail, the disappointment can shatter our confidence and strongly affect the rest of our life. As long as competition causes us to exploit our abilities, genuine accomplishment becomes blocked by frustration and failure.

If we were to emphasize cooperation rather than competition, we would naturally feel more secure, more confident in our abilities, and we would feel less need to win at the expense of others. But we cling to familiar ways; we compete believing that this is the accepted way to do things, no matter what the consequences may be.

When we examine the role of competition in our work, and the effect it has on our lives, we can see how it is often our fears and disappointments that spur us to compete. It is useful to take the time to look back over your past, considering the different forms of competition that you have entered into. How much pressure was there on you to win? Were you afraid of failing? Remember how you felt when you won, and when you lost. When you won, did you care about those who lost? When you see how competition has affected you, you can understand that others have the same feelings you have experienced. You will see that competition usually causes pain for everyone involved, and you can use this insight to develop more compassion for others and for yourself.

It is not easy, however, to give up the glow of success and ego-gratification, even if we know it is superficial and short-lived. But if we are genuinely concerned with our personal growth and with finding ways to improve our lives, then we must apply this concern to all our relationships: to co-workers, family, and friends. As we learn to treat others with more caring, and as we learn to be more honest with ourselves, competing to win loses its hold on us. It falls away before our growing strength, defeated by human understanding and sharing. As we learn more about the real nature of humanity, we come closer to the source of true human values. Those around us respond to our strength and knowledge with openness and appreciation, and instead of competing to win we can help each other to grow.

We can enjoy our successes in life, and find fulfillment in healthy competition if we balance the pleasure of success with a willingness to appreciate and learn from our failures as well. This means that when we do the best we can, even if we fail, we can be grateful for the experience, for it can reveal to us where we can improve our abilities. Rather than approaching a competitive event as something of major importance, we can look on it with humility, and allow it to teach us to know ourselves better. We no longer have to fear failure, for we can see that the worst outcome is not failure, but our disappointment in ourselves.

When we relieve the pressure caused by disappointment and a fear of failure, work and life become rich and fulfilling. There is no reason to allow such pressure to shape our lives; we can learn instead to live and work cooperatively. Our work will be smoother, more meaningful, and rewarding. Our sense of satisfaction in life will deepen and we can share our appreciation with others. As we influence others to support one another, we will find our own appreciation growing stronger, and our understanding more profound.

Just as competition encourages more competition, so cooperation inspires love and caring in those who feel it and receive it. When we see all others as friends in a mutual search for fulfillment, we share in the richness of human experience. When all of us work together rather than competing in useless and narrow ways, the possibilities for genuine support and caring are infinite.

PART THREE

Sharing

When we invest our care in others, our positive feelings grow and spread; others respond with their love, and the richness of this shared experience uplifts the quality of life everywhere. Our care and joy grow stronger, and we increase our ability to deepen and expand our true concern for others. When we base our lives on caring, our relationships have a sound and healthy foundation, and we have the strength to deal skillfully with anything that arises.

How to Use
Our Human Resources

We would all get more out of work and life if we had less. This does not mean that we should give everything away and try to live on nothing, or that we should feel guilty about enjoying what we have. It means that there is a beauty to living and working with precision and efficiency, to taking only what we need. This brings inner balance, a sense of peaceful attunement with everything around us. But this immediate connection to values, this clarity about what we really need, can be obscured when we have too much.

Even though our possessions seldom satisfy us in a lasting way, we tend to think that owning many things is what appreciating life is all about. Our lives become cluttered with possessions, and though occasionally we may get rid of some of the things we never use, soon we are busy replacing what was thrown away.

This attitude toward goods and possessions is constantly reinforced by our culture. We feel subtle pressure from our friends, our families, and those we work with, to 'keep up' our material standard of living. Because of the abundance and prosperity all around us, we are encouraged to act out a pattern of excess in our lives. Though we may worry about the destruction of our forests and the desolation of nature, we forget that much of the waste of resources and energy is being carried out to fulfill our demands. Even those who decry the wasteful practices of our culture would admit, if they were honest, that they have many more possessions than they need.

Although possessions can enrich our experience and be of use to us as we live and work in the world, when we become attached to them, they take on too much importance in our lives. We begin to think that the more we have, the more satisfaction will be ours. We lose sight of the fact that what actually gives us satisfaction is not these things themselves, but the way in which we use them. Our desire to own things leads to a selfish, grasping attitude which causes us to lose our sense of balance with the world, and insulates us from change and growth.

As our desires become centered around ourselves, we get caught up in patterns of needing and wanting. Frustration accompanies this self-serving frame of mind; when we do not get what we want, a feeling of loss and resentment arises. When we *do* manage to get what we want, we must then protect and defend it. Either way, we are on a limited and narrow path which closes us off from others.

The constant excess and misuse of our resources can dull our sense of the difference between real and extraneous needs. We come to value things for the short term, to think only of enjoyment and convenience, and fail to take a broader perspective. We grow out of touch with the basic values of life, and end up forgetting the many who never have enough. If we were close enough to truly feel another's needs, every one of us would give help. But when our values are clouded, when we are insulated by a cushion of material comfort, it is hard to perceive, much less respond to, the needs and difficulties of others.

When we recognize what our wasteful habits do to our lives, to our work, to our relationships, we can come to know our real needs more clearly. We stop responding so readily to our superficial desires, and are able to concentrate our energies on the things that are truly meaningful to us, the things that make our lives worth living.

In order to keep in touch with our values, it is helpful periodically to look closely at the ways we use our possessions. Spend a few minutes to consider all that you own. How much do you really need? How much do you actually use? How much do you waste? If you have more than you can use, do you share what you have with others? When you plan to acquire something new, keep these questions in mind. They will help you to take a more responsible view toward what you plan to acquire and how you will use it.

Perhaps there has already begun a turning back in our culture toward basic, simple values, an effort to apply traditional ideals and virtues to modern life. We are also beginning to keep more of an eye on the future, preserving our resources for the use of generations to come. This change is very encouraging, for as a leading nation, we set an example to the rest of the world. As we move increasingly toward a wiser, more economic use of resources and energy, perhaps others will be influenced by these positive changes, and come together to share in finding ways to use all of our resources well.

But this is still only a future possibility. First we must make this change real in our personal lives, in our ways of working and living. We need to be aware of how we use things, and learn to use them well. At work, when we know just what is needed, no more and no less, we move fluidly, each step well thought out. We are careful with materials, time, and energy; planning is smooth, and unanticipated problems are dealt with easily. Each moment is full of vitality and interest, and we feel an immediate connection with whatever we do. Co-workers come together into a team, sharing problems and pleasures. We enjoy a clear sense of purpose, and we derive real satisfaction and meaning from our work.

As we learn to apply economy to all areas of our life, freeing ourselves from the jumble of waste and inefficiency, we grow self-reliant and stable, and come to view our lives with greater clarity. We learn to appreciate our inner resources, our strengths as well as our weaknesses, and our new clarity gives us further opportunities to change our attitudes and our negative patterns. Instead of worrying about not having enough, threatened by a future empty of meaning, we enjoy the promise of steady growth and contentment, a vision of the fullness of life's true values.

Self-Knowledge

We come to know the beauty of human nature by recognizing the truth and integrity of our own being. This recognition lends clarity to our perceptions, strength to our decisions and actions, and a profound sense of security to our lives. By knowing who we really are, we release the joy, the truth, and the deep appreciation that lie within each of us. Genuine self-knowledge enables us to guide our lives in healthy and meaningful directions, touching all of our experience with the strength of awareness.

Knowing ourselves well improves the quality of life, yet many of us find it difficult to realize this liberating self-knowledge. We may spend a good portion of our lives seeking our true identity, trying different vocations, making new friends, searching for new activities to capture our interest. Yet often, the more we look for ourselves in these things, the more confusing all experience seems to be.

What is it that prevents us from discovering the truth of our inner being? Each of us has a self-image that is based on who we think we are and how we think others see us. When we look in a mirror, we know that what we see there is only a reflection; even though our self-image has the same illusory quality, we often believe it to be real. Our belief in this image draws us away from the true qualities of our nature.

The self-image is like a mirage; it promises us nourishment, but when a problem arises which demands the strength of a clear and self-confident mind, the self-image has nothing to offer; it fails to sustain us when we most need support. Because the self-image is based on how we wish we were, on what we fear we are, or how we would like the world to see us, it prevents us from seeing ourselves clearly. We fail to recognize both our true strengths and many of our faults.

The self-image is particularly deceptive because it can blind us to our weaknesses and shortcomings. By recognizing these qualities we could begin to change them, but when we rely on our self-image to cover them over, we obstruct our growth. We use our self-image to avoid looking at ourselves honestly, creating a prideful picture of ourselves that allows us to believe our shortcomings are only minor problems. Or we may dwell on our negative qualities and limit ourselves by hiding behind a self-deprecating image.

When we direct our energy to supporting our self-image, we also prevent ourselves from relating openly to others. We may grow deaf to feedback which does not conform to our view of ourselves, or discredit the truth when it is pointed out to us. Although we may succeed by these actions in manipulating others to support our image, by cutting ourselves off from honest criticism, we lose touch with those who actually care to help us. We also grow more distant from the inner knowledge which can help us to discriminate the truth in what others say. With nothing to rely on, no stable ground on which to stand, we cling even more tightly to our concepts of ourselves.

How can we move beyond the limitations of the self-image and come to know ourselves more truly? We can begin by looking closely at who we think we are. Take the time to carefully examine how you appear to yourself. How are you and your self-image related? As you continue to look at your concepts about yourself, see how they relate to those you work with, your family, and friends; observe how you appear to others. Although tracking your self-image is not easy, when you begin to see your concepts about yourself more clearly, you can lighten their hold on your life. You can look at yourself more honestly, and learn to recognize and accept all of your qualities, all of your positive traits as well as all of your faults.

You can then increase your self-awareness and your self-confidence by looking carefully at the patterns of growth in your life. Look at all that you have accomplished, and the qualities that have affected your growth. Seeing that you have overcome problems and corrected past mistakes can encourage you to view future problems as opportunities to learn. You can build up your self-knowledge and confidence the same way an athlete builds up his physical skills: though at first seeing yourself may be difficult, exercising your growing strength becomes a pleasure as your self-image gives way to true self-knowledge. Viewing your strengths and weaknesses with clarity leads to a true confidence in yourself; your growing awareness becomes a source of strength in your work and your life, a ground on which to stand.

As we work to increase our awareness, we must go through a process of development, a process which is delicate and needs careful nurturing. While we are looking into ourselves, expanding our willingness to examine both our strengths and weaknesses, and beginning to take steps to change, we may not be sure of our ground. Yet we may be tempted to test our growing knowledge of ourselves by talking about what we are going through, or attempting to advise others. When we talk about a process of inner growth before we have fully integrated it, we risk losing what we have gained. We tend to dissipate the strength of our awareness, substituting talk for the growth itself.

A child runs to mother with a bubble, and is disappointed when it bursts before he can reach her. When we attempt to share our awareness too soon, we are often similarly disappointed and disillusioned. We may find that other people misunderstand what we tell them; or they may not really care about what we have to say. They may ridicule us, denying the validity of our views and causing us to doubt ourselves. When this occurs, we may lose our confidence, and even our ability to touch our deeper and more sensitive thoughts and feelings.

Moreover, the energy we put into talking about ourselves is valuable energy that could be applied to increasing our awareness. When we use our energy wisely, it can help us go deeper into ourselves, and make the changes we need to make. Gradually we become more aware of the qualities which lead to growth, and as we continue to grow, we protect our development naturally. When we have fully digested and incorporated our growing strength, then we can share it with others.

Encouragement from others is often helpful, but more important is the encouragement we give to ourselves. When we deal with the person we really are, we gain confidence; nobody can shake us from our foundation. When we are in touch with reality, we are not weakened by anything in life. As we see our strength grow, and learn the confidence that comes from knowing our inner nature, we develop clarity and honesty, as well as awareness.

When we are truly aware of ourselves, we know where we stand, we know who we are. We are willing to accept both our accomplishments and our shortcomings, and the lessons they can teach us. We recognize the potential in all experience to enrich our lives, and we make use of everything that happens to grow and develop in healthier ways.

We gain a balanced view of our relationship to ourselves and to others. As we come to appreciate who we really are, we begin to appreciate the qualities of others, and our understanding of human nature deepens. Accepting ourselves and accepting others then becomes easy; when we are confident in ourselves, we can open our hearts to include everyone else in our lives. Our environment is lightened by the caring and compassion that spring from this natural acceptance. Our energy and our work are directed by clarity, by a clear sense of who we are and what we want to achieve. The results of our work, and the developing meaning of life, lead to an ever greater appreciation and stability in everything we do.

Communication

Communication is the vital link between our visions and the support needed to help them take form. It preserves the most valuable insights of mankind, carrying both the inspiration that sparks creativity, and the truth that expresses the fullness of human nature. It provides the means for transmitting knowledge from one generation to the next. Thus communication plays a crucial role in the ongoing process of improving the quality of life.

When we truly communicate, we open channels of love and caring, inspiring openness in one another, and awakening a deep appreciation of the joy and meaning in life. In whatever we are trying to communicate, our genuine caring is always part of the message, for true communication creates one heart, one mind, uniting us in a common bond of friendship and mutual understanding. Thoughts and feelings are expressed smoothly and clearly; our minds, hearts, and energy are totally involved, merged in a flowing unity.

Good working relationships depend on this flowing interaction. When we truly care about working together, we know the importance of understanding and being understood, of being clear and honest in what we say and how we say it. We listen to and support each other, and problems in our work are dealt with smoothly. We help each other willingly, accomplishing our goals together, sharing all of our energy. We are sensitive to the internal messages from our own feelings and thoughts, and therefore we are also sensitive to the people we work with. A natural harmony and caring result when we communicate well.

Most of us, however, are out of touch with the inner knowledge that is the essence of communication. Rather than being open to ourselves and able to share our thoughts and feelings, we become concerned with protecting our self-image. Though we say we want to communicate, our gestures and expressions, our tone of voice, and the momentum of our speech may reveal that we do not really wish to share. Unless we know ourselves well and clearly understand both our motivation and our message, we often communicate little more than confusion.

When we have no real interest in sharing, no meaningful exchange of ideas can take place. We may state our views only partially, and expect the other person to fully understand what we have said. Or we may couch our concepts in language that few can penetrate. Though others do not understand, they may accept our position and ideas without question, simply to hide their lack of understanding. In this way we use communication to manipulate others rather than as a means of opening to them. The opportunity for the flow and sharing of ideas, the opportunity to deepen our human understanding, is lost.

If we do not care enough to communicate well, all we can truly communicate is our lack of caring. When we closely examine our patterns of communication, taking into consideration how others react to what we say, we will begin to see how our lack of caring hinders our efforts to communicate clearly. We will see if we are truly listening to what the other person has to say, or whether we are more concerned with making our own views known. Noting whether we interrupt or whether we are willing to look directly at another person can tell us much about our true motivation.

By observing our interactions with others, we can understand the problems in communication we create for ourselves. If we want to realize the satisfaction of sharing with others, we must develop our willingness to openly communicate with those around us. In order to do this, we must resolve to change with the full force of our hearts and minds. Once we have done this, we can ensure that our caring is always a clear part of our message.

As we open our hearts more to others, we see that listening well means opening all of our senses to hear what others have to say, not only in their words but in their hearts. In this way we come to truly understand how others feel, and what they have to tell us. This responsiveness allows us to open more deeply to ourselves, and communication becomes a bridge to human understanding. As we begin to communicate with honesty, our ideas and our perspectives develop, change, and grow, and we discover a deep sense of satisfaction in our interactions with others.

The mutual respect and recognition which grow from true communication are far more satisfying and enduring than praise or admiration of our superficial qualities. When we relax and open to ourselves and others, when we stop trying to protect ourselves and our ideas, we begin to make positive changes in our lives. When we calmly and meditatively interrelate with the world around us, we find that we can clearly communicate our ideas, and our goals naturally come into being. We are in tune with the world and the world is in tune with us.

Living in a harmonious relationship with the world enhances the development of knowledge and creativity in our lives, and in the lives of those around us. The need to maintain a self-image vanishes, for others appreciate us for who we really are, and we in turn appreciate all those around us. Learning to communicate well brings a deep peace and joy to our lives. Our relationships with co-workers, family, and friends grow warm and lasting, for they are grounded in truth and caring.

Cooperation

The ability to work well with others grows out of the qualities that contribute to healthy living: stability, honesty, clarity, inner confidence, and well-focused awareness. As we develop these qualities, we learn to share our skills and experience with others, and this is the beginning of cooperation. As we care for and help others with an open heart, we discover that they respond to us in a mutually supportive way.

Working well with others produces both an awareness of the unique value of each individual, and an appreciation for the synthesis that is produced when many individuals participate in a task. Cooperation releases a vital force of creative energy which can bring about far greater benefits that any individual could achieve alone. Progress, both on an individual and global level, depends on this cooperation.

But even though each of us can appreciate the value of cooperation, we may not find it easy to work well with others. One of the common obstacles to cooperation is our tendency to think that our own feelings and attitudes are more important than those of others. We may think that we can do better on our own, directing our energies solely towards our own goals. We do not see that this self-centered view can affect both ourselves and others on many different levels.

While at first we may seem to do well, we gradually become closed down and isolated. We do not share information that is helpful to others' work. We foster petty jealousies which lead to resentment, and personal conflicts begin to take root and grow. Minor disputes become major problems, until finally, working well with others becomes difficult, if not impossible. Without cooperation to bring us together, our work and our relationships suffer, and we lose sight of the delights and benefits of working closely with each other.

An inability to cooperate is often the result of patterns of behavior formed in childhood, self-centered efforts to get our own way and avoid what we do not want. These patterns may rise to the surface in the way we deal with current problems in work, or in relationships that are going badly. We can be so concerned about our own interests that we ignore the importance of our interrelationships with others. Therefore, we close ourselves off from the essential elements of cooperation: looking outward, opening, and especially, caring.

We may try to be a little more open at home, but particularly at work we close off from the people we work with, from the work, and even from ourselves. In order to achieve our aims or to protect our self-image, we may try to manipulate those around us. We may hold to a position, refusing to cooperate, because we fear that if we let go and open to others, our weaknesses will be exposed. Yet this clinging to our selfish view is what prevents us from realizing our potential for caring and for working smoothly with those around us. We fail to see that cooperation is far more important than the successful defense of a point of view.

When we are willing to learn to cooperate, we open our lives to the rich experience of working well with others. The next time you have a conflict with someone you work with, rather than focusing on your feelings of anger or hurt, look for a positive solution to the problem. This is the time to let go of your emotions and try to work together, so that although there is disagreement, you can maintain a bond of cooperation. To do this, you may need to sacrifice the opportunity to give vent to your feelings—to 'win' your argument. But if you can loosen up and become more flexible in your interactions with others, you will set your natural creativity free to uplift the quality of your work, deepening the caring and understanding you have for those you work with.

To be able to truly cooperate with those around us, we also need to open to ourselves—to our bodies, our minds, our senses, and our feelings. When we recognize the messages we receive from these sources, our inner knowledge forms a bridge between ourselves and others.

We gain a broader view which encourages the development of positive, supportive relationships. We learn to be sensitive to moods and feelings; we know and care how others feel. We take note of their tone of voice or the momentum of their energy, and thus sense when and how to approach others with consideration. As we develop clearer perceptions and become more sensitive to others, our communication becomes more open and honest.

When we take the time to share knowledge and experience with our friends and co-workers, they are encouraged to do well, and to develop their abilities. Work is smoother and more efficient when we communicate clearly and provide honest feedback, when we support each other in expressing our ideas and in making decisions. We feel a common bond with those we work with, yet unique characteristics are valued; problems are worked out smoothly, and working energies become balanced. In this way, we grow to trust one another and develop a strong loyalty to the concerns of our work.

As the working environment becomes vital and productive—conducive to growth, honesty, clarity, and cooperation—these qualities are incorporated into all that we do. We become fully willing to share in the work. We come to rely on each other, helping one another to overcome obstacles so that work flows evenly and enjoyably for all. We join all of our energies and ideas to create a strong and dynamic force that can accomplish goals too difficult for us to reach alone. Working together becomes an experience of mutual understanding and respect, a source of unlimited satisfaction, and a creative inspiration for everyone.

The quality of everything we do is uplifted when we express a natural caring for others. When we let go of our self-centered views, and work with an open mind, in harmony with those around us, we will begin to experience a deep joy and satisfaction in all of our interactions. Our growth will be accelerated by our open-minded perspective, and we will see a decline in the problems and conflicts not only in our own lives, but in our entire culture. Thus the benefits of cooperation lighten the quality of life for all humanity.

Caring and cooperation reveal to us the many pleasures of work, and the time we spend at work becomes a source of stimulation and enjoyment. Challenges are welcomed, and creative potential expands both at work and elsewhere. Energy is positive and cheerful, and overflows into the rest of life; distinctions between work and spare time diminish as work is integrated into a harmonious approach to living. When we learn to truly cooperate, there is no limit to what we can accomplish, to how deeply we can enjoy our lives.

Responsibility

It is a simple matter to recognize our personal responsibilities: we all have certain duties to fulfill, certain obligations to be met. These are clear to us. But our responsibilities are not limited to our personal duties, for in a much deeper sense, we are responsible for our total experience: for how we relate to the world at large.

True responsibility is an active caring and responsiveness to everything around us, a readiness to do whatever needs to be done. This means that we take responsibility not only for certain obligations, but for every aspect of life, responding to each experience with a dynamic willingness, an openness to life that springs from a deep caring.

To develop responsibility, we need mindfulness, the knowledge of how things actually are. This means being aware: aware of our actions and thoughts, aware of their effects on others, and even aware of their consequences on a global level. This awareness allows us to always respond appropriately, to open to the true needs of the people around us, and to act spontaneously in ways that create harmony and balance.

We each have the capacity for this responsiveness and awareness, but most of us have not been taught to develop it. Traditionally, education has been the process of learning both the knowledge and skills to take a truly responsible place in the world. But today, education usually provides only information, and fails to teach us to use it well in our lives. We do not know the true nature and extent of our responsibility as human beings.

We need to develop a 'higher education' which is rooted in caring and founded on respect for knowledge and experience. Although it is not easy to find such an education today, we can look to the traditional values of the past, for they transmit the knowledge accumulated by all who have come before us. This is the treasure which we inherit, and if we learn to use it well, we will gain from it the knowledge of how to act effectively in the world.

Work gives us the opportunity to educate ourselves, to incorporate higher values into our daily experience. By caring for our work, responding fully to it, we can begin to understand the nature of our responsibility as human beings. For we have a responsibility to work, to exercise our talents and abilities, to contribute our energy to life. Our nature is creative, and by expressing it, we constantly generate more enthusiasm and creativity, stimulating an ongoing process of enjoyment in the world around us. Working willingly, with our full energy and enthusiasm, is our way of contributing to life.

Every kind of work can be a pleasure. Even simple household tasks can be an opportunity to exercise and expand our caring, our effectiveness, our responsiveness. As we respond with caring and vision to all work, we develop our capacity to respond fully to all of life. Every action generates positive energy which can be shared with others. These qualities of caring and responsiveness are the greatest gift we have to offer.

When we do not respond to our work with our full energy, we limit our potential, and deny our true nature. Instead of contributing fully to life, being responsible for our creative nature, we set limits on what we can do. When our work does not go well, we may claim we have too much responsibility, or that responsibility was thrust upon us; we may try to blame our ineffectiveness on our lack of experience. Furthermore, because we have not cared enough to put all of our energy into our work, we do not actually consider ourselves responsible for the results we produce.

When we do not participate fully in our work, we deprive our families, our society, and our world of the full expression of our energy. This resistance to our responsibility as human beings may take many forms. We may think that because we have enough money to support ourselves, we do not need to work. We may approach our work as a duty, a forceful obligation we fulfill against our will. We may work only for money. Whatever the case, when we view our work as something to be resisted rather than as an opportunity to be fully used, we actually take advantage of all other beings in the universe; we take advantage of life itself. We have the gift of life, and if we do not use it fully, we create an imbalance in the world, for others must support us with their energy.

Our history shows clearly the effects of self-centered, irresponsible action. Broken agreements, social conflicts, and ecological disasters, all indicate a failure to take genuine responsibility, a failure to respond fully and with awareness to the demands of life. We have all seen those who have led others into difficulties or danger and then have refused to accept responsibility for their actions. Those who follow are also responsible, however, for whether we are leading or being led, we are responsible for what is done.

If we fail to insist that those who guide us prove their integrity or show responsible action, we prepare the way for thoughtless guidance in the future. When we listen to those who promise us what we want to hear, instead of to those with the knowledge and experience to lead us well, we foster a general lack of responsiveness and caring.

If we are to act with responsibility, we need to strengthen our feelings of caring. We can then make an effort to see our situation from a wider perspective. When we become more responsive to those around us, to our work, to those we work with, we gain a clearer sense of the possible effects of our actions. As our awareness and capacity for responsiveness expand, we find we are able to take full responsibility for the future welfare of our children, our community, and our world.

Looking to our personal past can help us to develop our capacity for caring. We can all remember a time when we responded openly and fully to another, considering his needs as our own. Take the time to remember the details of this memory: what happened, how you felt about the other person, what you did.

Then turn your attention to a memory of a time when you did not act with caring, when your words or actions were hurtful to someone else. Carefully review the situation, examining your motives and actions, your responses to the other person. Remember if you thought about his feelings before you acted; note what you were concerned with. When you have reviewed this situation as thoroughly as you can, imagine responding to it with the full power of your caring, and allow your positive feelings to grow stronger in your heart.

Acting responsibly stimulates healthy growth and positive attitudes, and therefore lends a purpose to our lives. We live in a natural way, in step with the rhythms of the universe, with a deep caring for whatever we do. As we grow to understand the nature of existence, we see that ultimately it is the truth for which we are responsible. Though sometimes a lonely position on which to stand, it is the truth that will liberate us from selfishness, resentment, fear, and anxiety. When we take responsibility in our lives to pursue the truth and stand behind it, we find our existence strengthened by it. The truth clarifies our perspective, and directs us on a healthy path of growth and fulfillment. Given the foundation of responsibility, time and knowledge open us to the infinite possibilities of existence. Although we may falter at first, if we continue to encourage ourselves, we gain true freedom.

Responsible action comes naturally once it has been developed. We are not burdened by a sense of duty or obligation—we act responsibly because it is the natural, healthy way to be. We live in accordance with a caring, responsive relationship to the world. This responsiveness is as complete as the responsiveness of the sun to the earth, an unbroken agreement fulfilled without hesitation.

Humility

True humility is not easy to attain these days. At most levels of life, subtle dishonesty, competition, and selfishness prevail, and we have lost touch with the value of sharing with others. We hold back our love and concern, and keep our joyful feelings to ourselves because we are afraid to share. Joy may come so rarely into our lives, and others' needs may seem so overwhelming, that we feel we should keep what we can for ourselves. Thus we fail to nurture the qualities of love and caring that would enhance our relationships with others.

When we develop the resources of our inner nature, when we actively share our warmth and joy, this inspires others to develop similar feelings, and we discover the great richness and value that we can receive from one another. This open sharing with others is an expression of true humility.

Humility is an experience of the commonality of all human beings. It leads to a balanced outlook on human nature that takes into account all the strengths and failings each of us is subject to. To be truly humble requires taking an honest look at ourselves, and coming to clearly know our abilities and weaknesses. When our personal evaluation is honest, we can respect who we are, and this deep acceptance of our nature leads to a wider understanding and greater respect for others. We are motivated to help others with their problems and to support them in cultivating their capabilities. We see that we all share similar goals of happiness and fulfillment; we are all subject to similar problems and difficulties.

When we are not honest with ourselves, we cannot respect our inherent nature, so we rely on our self-image to give us a sense of worth. We become so concerned with protecting ourselves that we begin to see only our selfish objectives; if others are hurt by our actions, we do not truly care. As our perspective narrows, we forget the fundamental dignity of every human being. We lose respect for others and begin to feel that we are superior to everyone else.

This pride is actually a sign of our lack of self-confidence and self-respect. Because we cannot accept our shortcomings, we maintain a false view of ourselves; our pride then leads to inconsiderateness and estrangement from others. We compete with those around us in order to have things the way we think they should be; we point out others' faults and mistakes and ignore their virtues and abilities. But our comparisons and judgments, rather than proving our worth, only expose our lack of self-knowledge and widen the gulf that stands between us and our humanity. Until we ourselves are free from fault, we are not in a position to criticize others, for we continually make mistakes, usually the same ones we condemn.

Everyone has faults, obstacles to positive achievement. When we are aware of these faults in ourselves, it is difficult to maintain a superior attitude toward others. As we grow to be more honest, and willingly admit our shortcomings, we increase our self-knowledge and self-respect. This self-respect overcomes our fears of inadequacy, and we no longer feel the need to act superior. It is even possible to allow ourselves to fail, and thereby accept the opportunity failure can give us to learn from our mistakes. As our increasing self-awareness leads to greater awareness of human nature, we become concerned for others' welfare, and this caring quality creates true humility.

Developing a humble attitude can transform our selfish tendencies into generosity, and we can then discover the beauty of true giving and sharing with others. As we allow a deep caring to permeate all of our actions, we realize that the humble heart is the greatest heart of all. The respect and concern we show to others awaken in them a mutual recognition and warmth, and all of our interactions are elevated to a vital level.

You can develop your awareness and sense of caring by looking honestly at yourself and your relationships with others. A good place to start is to examine your attitudes toward someone you dislike. Look carefully at each of the qualities in this person that annoy you. Are they qualities you do not like in yourself?

The next time you see this person, focus on one of his positive qualities and allow a good feeling towards him to grow in your heart. From this time on nurture this feeling and do not let any negative judgments pull you off balance. After a few weeks or months, check back to see how your feelings about this person have changed. When you continue this process with everyone you dislike, you will discover that there is no one alive you could not care for deeply.

When we invest our care in others, our positive feelings grow and spread; others respond with their love, and the richness of this shared experience uplifts the quality of life everywhere. Our care and joy grow stronger, and we increase our ability to deepen and expand our true concern for others. When we base our lives on caring, our relationships have a sound and healthy foundation, and we have the strength to deal skillfully with anything that arises.

This kind of humility is the greatest treasure of life. When we respond to one another with caring and love, there are no separations between us. We no longer get caught in conflicts, for we see that our differences express our unique qualities, inspiring a deep appreciation of human nature. As we experience the full commonality of all human beings, our attitude toward life becomes light and open. We discover that participating with others in a mutual sharing of knowledge and experience generates the wisdom to fulfill all needs, and to live in harmony with all beings. This discovery, this expression of true humility, is one of the most valuable insights we can attain.

Index

About the Author

Tarthang Tulku Rinpoche is a religious teacher from Tarthang Monastery in East Tibet. During his early life in Tibet he received a thorough education in the philosophy and practice of Tibetan Buddhism from some of the greatest spiritual teachers of the East. In 1959 he left Tibet and went to India where he taught at Sanskrit University in Benares for seven years. It was at this time that he founded Dharmamudranalaya, a press dedicated to the preservation of Tibetan literature.

Upon coming to the United States in 1968, Tarthang Tulku began the challenging task of establishing the Dharma in America. In 1969 he founded the Tibetan Nyingma Meditation Center, and this religious organization became the ground from which the Nyingma Centers grew. Here many students have come to work, study, and practice under Rinpoche's guidance, entering a path of spiritual development that takes all experience as a source of growth and awareness.

Dharma Publishing and Dharma Press, founded in 1971, have created over fifty titles in Buddhist studies.

Rinpoche has authored several of these works, including *Time, Space and Knowledge, Gesture of Balance, Openness Mind, Kum Nye Relaxation, Parts One and Two,* and *Skillful Means.* In addition, he has edited several volumes, among them the *Crystal Mirror* series (five volumes) and has supervised the translations of some of the more important Buddhist texts that have been published.

At the Nyingma Institute of Berkeley, established in 1973, Rinpoche has played a vital role in the meeting of East and West. Psychologists, health professionals, educators, and students from all over the world have come to study and apply the teachings of the Nyingma tradition within the context of their own lives and professions. Rinpoche has taught many courses in both philosophy and meditation to several thousand students in the past six years. In 1973, he initiated the Human Development Training Program, a dynamic integration of Eastern approaches to healthful living with the psychology of the West.

In 1975 Rinpoche began work on Odiyan, the Nyingma country retreat center in Northern California. He has closely supervised all aspects of planning, construction, and development in this monumental project, and as Odiyan now nears completion its beauty reflects the clarity and depth of Rinpoche's vision. Odiyan will be a permanent home for the Dharma in America, a center for the preservation of Tibetan culture and tradition.

Here, Americans will have the opportunity to live in the healthful environment of this spiritual community, realizing the truths of the Dharma in their daily lives. Translation of Tibetan texts will be an important future activity, and the opportunity will be available, to any who are sincerely interested, to study and practice the teachings of the Nyingma tradition.

In addition to these major centers, Rinpoche has also founded several other organizations. The Tibetan Nyingma Relief Foundation has provided assistance to Tibetan refugees in India, Nepal, and Bhutan since 1971. The Nyingma Institutes of Phoenix, Arizona and Boulder, Colorado bring the teachings of the Nyingma tradition to a steadily growing number of students in the United States.

Lama Anagarika Govinda, one of the well-known authorities on Tibetan Buddhism, has said of Tarthang Tulku's activities: "It is indeed something of a miracle that you, who arrived in this country as a penniless refugee, have been able to achieve in seven years, what all the Buddhists in Europe have not been able to achieve in seventy years: namely to create a self-sufficient Buddhist community with facilities for studying and practicing the Dharma in all its aspects. . . ."

It *is* remarkable that a man from so remote a country as Tibet would have such relevant insights to offer modern Western culture. The traditional Dharma teachings are not readily accessible to the West for they are expressed in a language and context that are unfamiliar to Westerners. In working with Americans over the past ten years, Rinpoche has explored many ways to express the truths of his tradition in a practical form that has relevance to Western culture. In Rinpoche's books, these profound truths speak directly to the Western mind and heart. The results of his work and experience confirm the deep value that *Skillful Means* holds for all who read it.

Other Dharma Publishing Books

Time, Space, and Knowledge: A New Vision of Reality by Tarthang Tulku. Thirty-five exercises and a rigorous philosophical text reveal ever more brilliant times, spaces, and knowledges.

Kum Nye Relaxation, Parts 1 and 2 by Tarthang Tulku. Over 200 exercises for discovering the relaxing energies within our bodies and senses.

Gesture of Balance by Tarthang Tulku. The Nyingma method of meditation wherein all life experience is meditation.

Openness Mind by Tarthang Tulku. The sequel to *Gesture of Balance*, with more advanced meditation techniques.

Kindly Bent to Ease Us by Longchenpa. A translation of Longchenpa's guide to the Dzogchen path to enlightenment.

The Life and Liberation of Padmasambhava by Yeshe Tsogyal. A translation of the complete biography of Tibetan Buddhism's founder. Two volumes, 58 color plates.

Crystal Mirror Series edited by Tarthang Tulku. Introductory exploration of the various aspects of Tibetan philosophy, history, psychology, art, and culture. Five volumes currently available.

Calm and Clear by Lama Mipham. Translations of two beginning meditation texts by a brilliant 19th century Tibetan Lama.

If you order Dharma books directly from the publisher, it will help us to make more such books available. Write for a free catalog and new book announcements.

Dharma Publishing, 2425 Hillside Avenue
Berkeley, California 94704 USA